LAW
BASICS
Student Study Guides

EUROPEAN UNION

FIFTH EDITION

LAW
BASICS
Student Study Guides

EUROPEAN UNION

FIFTH EDITION

By

Alan S. Reid, LLB (Hons), Dip LP, LLM

Senior Lecturer in EU law, Sheffield Hallam University

W. GREEN THOMSON REUTERS

First Edition published 2002
Second Edition published 2004
Third Edition published 2007
Fourth Edition published 2010
Fifth Edition published 2013

(Registered in England &Wales, Company No.1679046.
Registered Office and address for service:
100 Avenue Road, London NW3 3PF
trading as W. Green)

Typeset by Alex Nashed, W. Green, Edinburgh.
Printed and bound in Great Britain by CPI Antony Rowe.

No natural forests were destroyed to make this product;
only farmed timber was used and re-planted.

A CIP catalogue record for this book is available from
the British Library.

ISBN 978-0-414-01928-7

Thomson Reuters and the Thomson Reuters logo
are trademarks of Thomson Reuters.

© 2013 Thomson Reuters (Legal) Limited

NOTE TO FIFTH EDITION

All topics included in the Fifth Edition have been updated to reflect the law as of July 1, 2013.

This edition is dedicated to the three most important girls in my life, Emma, Ellie and Ava.

Alan S. Reid
July 2013

CONTENTS

TABLE OF CASES

TABLE OF EUROPEAN LEGISLATION

Directives

TABLE OF UK STATUTES

1. INTRODUCTION

Students of European law face a daunting prospect. They are essentially studying an "alien" law, since the law of the European Union stems from a supranational legal and political system far removed from the comforting familiarity of domestic law. To a certain extent, students of EU law have to unlearn what they have been taught in other law classes. Upon studying EU law, students quickly realise that cherished and long-established constitutional principles such as Parliamentary Supremacy and Parliamentary Sovereignty have to cede to the European Union concept of the rule of law.

The law of the European Union is unique. The European Union legal system is sui generis, that is it is a unique legal system without precedent in legal history. It displays features of international law and that of national law and has created unique legal principles, as well as unique interpretations of pre-existing legal precepts. EU law has the power to override inconsistent domestic law and it can be used as both a shield and as a sword in domestic legal proceedings. EU law is designed to be practical and effective, even if at times it does not seem like it.

Nevertheless, it is important to note that further deepening of European cooperation and a widening of the EU's geography is work-in-progress. Indeed, the road to full European integration still lies ahead.

The Primary Law of the European Union:

The Treaty on the Functioning of the European Union	The Treaty on European Union	The Charter of Fundamental Rights	The EURATOM Treaty

2. FROM COMMUNITY TO UNION

The establishment and development of the European Union took place against the backdrop of conflict between European nation states. Incessant warfare had resulted in such devastation that, by the late 1940s, it was clear that it was no longer possible for nation states, particularly those European powers who still ruled over large colonial empires, to operate political and economic policies which did not involve their immediate neighbours. At the same time, apprehension over the ambitions of the Soviet Union, which by that time had occupied the Eastern part of Europe, impelled the democratic states of Western Europe and the United States of America to join in the North Atlantic Treaty Organisation ("NATO").

Although reconstruction of post-war Europe was under way by the end of the decade, aided in no small part by millions of dollars poured into Western Europe by the United States by way of grants and loans under the Marshall Plan, the threat of Soviet expansion prompted moves towards the creation of some form of mutual interdependence. The French statesmen, Jean Monnet and Robert Schuman, devised a plan for a partnership between France and Germany for the production of coal and steel within the framework of an organisation open to the participation of the other countries of Europe. The Schuman Declaration was adopted on May 9, 1950 (a day now celebrated within the Member States as "Europe Day"). In 1951 the Treaty of Paris was signed, bringing a European Coal and Steel Community (the "ECSC") into being in April 1952. It was anticipated that not only would this pooling of the entire European coal and steel production under an independent authority eliminate the potential for conflict between France and Germany but would provide a sound basis for economic unification and expansion in the future. Thus, from early on in the history of the European Community, it was clear that the Community would likely expand both geographically and substantively, as regards its spheres of competence.

The founders of the ECSC used the word "supranational" in the original Treaty to describe this independent authority. Although the Community had been created through an international treaty concluded between sovereign nations, the signatories were aware that they had created something very different from simply another international organisation. Not only did they accept mutual obligations, but they limited their own sovereign rights, transferring some of them to independent institutions over which they had no direct control and conferred on these institutions powers which they themselves did not possess. A legal system had been created to which the words "international" and "national" did not apply. The term "supranational" indicated that difference.

The European Coal and Steel Treaty then set up four institutions. These were based not on a rigid separation of powers, but on a community of interests. These institutions were:

- A High Authority formed by independent appointees of the Member States' governments, with responsibility for taking legally binding decisions and running the new Community. This body would act in the Community interest;
- a Council of Ministers made up of one representative from each of the Member States to represent the interests of those Member States (the signatories to the Treaty);
- an Assembly with delegates appointed by their respective nations' parliaments to represent the interests of the peoples of Europe; and
- a Court of Justice which would adjudicate on disputes and review the legality of the acts of the High Authority.

The signing of the European Coal and Steel Treaty in Paris on April 18, 1951 by the six founding countries (France, Germany, Italy, Belgium, Netherlands and Luxembourg) may be regarded as a first step towards European integration. Subsequently a European Atomic Power Community ("Euratom") was created by the Treaty of Rome signed on March 25, 1957. The intention was to create a specialist market for atomic energy, distribute it throughout the six countries who had signed the ECSC and sell on surpluses to non-Member States. Euratom shared the Assembly and Court of Justice with the ECSC but had its own Commission (similar in nature and functions to the ECSC's High Authority).

In 1956, "The Six" had also begun negotiations to set up another Community dealing with a wider range of economic matters. A second Rome Treaty signed on the same date as the Euratom Treaty brought the new Community into effect in 1958. It was entitled "The European Economic Community" ("EEC"). Its whole raison d'être was to establish and ensure the effective functioning of a common market based on free and fair competition and the abolition of trade barriers and as its preamble stated, "to lay the foundations of an ever closer union among the peoples of Europe". While the EEC had its own separate Commission and Council of Ministers, it shared the Assembly and Court of Justice with Euratom and the ECSC.

In contrast to the other two treaties, which as "traités loi" specified the exact powers of the institutions, the EEC Treaty was a "traité cadre", a framework treaty setting out general principles, leaving it to the institutions to work out policy and the detailed measures necessary to implement such policy. The initial steps towards achieving the goal of an efficient and effective common market involved the establishment of a customs union eliminating all customs duties and quotas between Member States and the creation of a common customs tariff for goods arriving from other non-Member States.

The aspirations of the founders were quite clear. They included:

- the formation of a supranational organisation;
- the creation and maintenance of a tariff-free market; and

- the development of a programme which would lead to the removal of all other national economic barriers throughout Europe, sector by sector, leading to deeper economic integration and one from which it would only be a short step to eventual political union.

By virtue of the Merger Treaty of 1965, the three Communities shared the same institutions under its common institutional framework. These institutions remained legally independent although their powers were derived from their respective Treaties. The Customs Union became fully operational by 1968. This meant that tariff and quota restrictions to trading between Member States had by then been abolished and that the replacement of national external tariffs by a common external tariff had been completed. However, by 1969 full freedom of movement had not yet been achieved in the markets for goods, persons, services and capital. Nor were the Community's institutions as effective as had been envisaged; decision making and legislation were taking place all too slowly. Throughout the 1970s there was pessimism about the future of the EEC. Economic crises on a global scale as well as internal political difficulties within the Member States of the Union had weakened the resolve of its members to press on with further integration. The first half of the 1970s saw the Community engage in its first enlargement. In 1973, Denmark, Ireland and the United Kingdom joined the European Community. The EC's second enlargement saw Greece join in 1981.

In 1985 several crucial events occurred which added impetus to the integration process for the 10 members of the EC. First, and outside of the EEC structure, the Benelux countries and France and Germany wished to abolish their internal border controls and strengthen their external borders. Thus, they signed an agreement to this effect at Schengen, Luxembourg.

Secondly, on January 1, 1985, Jacques Delors was appointed as the new President of the European Commission. With his encouragement, the UK Commissioner (Lord Cockfield) produced a detailed White Paper on the internal market which set the date of 1992 for elimination of the remaining barriers to trade. As the European Community could only act within the limits of the powers conferred upon it by the Treaties (which the Member States had signed and ratified) further modifications to its powers could only come about through amendment to these Treaties by way of Intergovernmental Conferences ("IGCs") of the Member States. Despite opposition from some Member States, an IGC took place, the outcome of which was the Single European Act of 1986. This Treaty, ratified by all Member States, was the single most important amendment to date of the EEC. It was comprised of two parts relating to its internal and external components. Its main features were to speed up the creation of a European economic market without internal frontiers and to reform all the main institutions of the Community to make them more effective, efficient and democratically accountable. This was to be achieved by:

- inauguration of the internal market programme which was to be completed by December 31, 1992;
- replacement of unanimity by qualified majority voting within the Council of Ministers for two-thirds of the 300 measures identified in the Cockfield White Paper as necessary to complete the internal market;
- creation of a cooperation procedure allowing the European Parliament enhanced participation in the legislative process by giving it a second reading of proposals;
- formalisation of the European Council (previously known as Summit Meetings between Heads of State and Government) as an organ of the European Community with increased policy-making authority;
- recognition of the Assembly as the European Parliament;
- creation of a Court of First Instance to ease the workload of the European Court of Justice;
- cooperation in an economic and monetary policy;
- common policies for research and technological development, and environment protection; and
- harmonisation in the areas of health, safety, consumer protection, professional and vocational qualifications, public procurement, VAT and excise duties, and frontier controls.

The second part of the Single European Act contained provisions for European Political Co-operation—that is, foreign policy co-operation between governments. The Act rekindled enthusiasm for integration.

In addition to the momentous changes wrought by the Single European Act, 1986 also saw the third enlargement of the EC. Accession of the Iberian Peninsula, that is Portugal and Spain, took EC membership to 12. At the beginning of the new decade, the population of the European Community also swelled, as a consequence of German reunification, adding a further 18 million people.

As a result of this renewed enthusiasm for integration, an ambitious IGC was convened and on February 7, 1992 the Treaty on European Union was signed by the 12 Member States. It brought into being a new legal entity—the European Union, comprising three pillars of European integration. Of the three pillars of the European Union created by the Treaty, the first and most important, was the European Communities pillar. This pillar comprised the three Communities which were established in the 1950s; the European Economic Community ("EEC"), the European Coal and Steel Community ("ECSC") and Euratom, and was supranational in nature, that is it was above the nation states. The other two pillars related to a Common Foreign and Security Policy (covering the political aspects of foreign policy as opposed to the economic aspects which were still within the Community pillar) and Justice and Home Affairs (amended by the Treaty of Amsterdam in 1997, to become Police and Judicial Co-operation in Criminal Matters). These latter two pillars involved intergovernmental co-operation only and permitted the promulgation of new secondary legislative acts such as common positions, joint positions, conventions and framework decisions.

As well as setting out a framework for the respective competences of the component parts of the Union, one of the central tenets of the Treaty was to set out detailed provisions for the organisation of Economic and Monetary Union ("EMU") and a timetable for its realisation.

Modifications were also made to the EEC Treaty (which was renamed the "EC Treaty") to amplify Community powers in some areas, attack what was widely perceived as a democratic deficit, strengthen the powers of the institutions and redress what appeared to be a widening gulf between the Community and its citizens.

The Treaty on European Union:

- set out a common institutional framework for all three pillars of the Union;
- introduced the principle of subsidiarity to its law-making process;
- created the status of Citizen of the European Union;
- introduced new, modified and expanded powers in the areas of economic and social cohesion (aid to less well-off regions), environmental protection, research and technological development, consumer protection, vocational training, the establishment and development of trans-European transport networks, public health protection, culture and development co-operation;
- changed the rules on the appointment of the Commission;
- Introduced a third reading stage for the European Parliament by way of a new co-decision procedure and extensions of the previous procedures;
- created the position of Ombudsman;
- introduced enhanced participation in European affairs by a Committee of the Regions; and
- created sanctions in the form of fines and/or periodic payments which could be levied by the Court of Justice in the event of a Member State failing to comply with its Community obligations. After complex negotiations during its passage and some considerable delay in ratifying it within the Member States thereafter, the Treaty on European Union entered into force in November 1993.

In 1995, the European Union saw its fourth enlargement, to 15 Member States, with the accession of Austria, Finland and Sweden. This year also saw the Schengen Agreement come into force.

The reforms agreed at Maastricht were widely perceived as disappointing, and disillusionment with Europe was increasingly reflected in public opinion. In particular, the unity of the Union system seemed to be under attack from two quarters. First, the expansion of European competences, although welcome, was achieved through intergovernmental co-operation in the second and third pillars and not through use of the supranational first pillar, thus undermining the entire ethos of European integration. Secondly, the provisions on flexibility which permitted some Member States to participate in certain policies whilst others lagged behind or opted out entirely, undermined European unity and threatened the creation of a two-tier Europe. Examples of this were the UK opt-out from the Social Policy chapter and the UK and Danish option on membership of Economic and Monetary Union. Accordingly the issues involved were quickly revisited and in 1996 a further IGC was convened with the aim of "ensuring the effectiveness of the mechanisms and the institutions of the Union". To some extent, progress was made:

- Some matters relating to visas, asylum, immigration and other policies relating to the free movement of persons were to be incorporated into the Community pillar instead of being located in the third pillar where they were subject only to intergovernmental co-operation procedures.
- The third pillar was renamed Police and Judicial Co-operation in Criminal Matters.
- An agreement on institutional reform to provide for enlargement did not materialise. Instead, the main point agreed was that Parliament's powers would be strengthened.
- Some Member States were to be provided with the means to move to closer integration between themselves in certain specified areas.
- Acts of the institutions could be reviewed by the Court of Justice to ensure their compliance with the principle of respect for human rights.
- Provision would be made for legislation to combat discrimination.
- Political control over a Member State guilty of certain serious and persistent breaches would be incorporated in a new treaty agreed by all existing Member States.

On May 1, 1999 the resultant Treaty of Amsterdam came into force. The existing Treaties were then amended accordingly. This involved not only altering their content, inserting new provisions and repealing old ones, but also re-numbering most of the previous provisions.

The year 1999 also saw the introduction of the single currency, the Euro, albeit in electronic (virtual) form only.

One of the most important issues that Amsterdam was supposed to resolve was the institutional position after enlargement. This matter was postponed during the IGC, and surfaced only in one of the Protocols to the Treaty of Amsterdam and several Declarations. At the European Council Cologne meeting in 1999, a further IGC was called. This IGC culminated in the adoption of the Treaty of Nice 2000, which entered into force on February 1, 2003. This Treaty dealt with most of the unfinished business of Amsterdam:

- As from January 1, 2005 the Commission was to comprise one national from each of the Member States. The Treaty of Nice also provided that after expansion of the Union to 27 Member States and beyond, the number of Commissioners was to be less than the number of Member States.
- The President of the Commission received increased powers concerning internal organisation of the Commission.
- Votes in the Council under Qualified Majority Voting were re-weighted. Qualified majority voting in the Council was extended in a number of policy fields, reducing the necessity for unanimity.
- Extension of the co-decision procedure for law-making within the Community, giving increased authority and responsibility to the European Parliament.
- An increase in size of the European Parliament. The Parliament was also elevated to the status of privileged applicant under the Action for Annulment procedure (see Ch.7, Judicial Review).
- The Council of Auditors comprises one representative from each Member State.
- Membership of the Economic and Social Committee and the Committee of the Regions was limited to 350 members each.
- Within the Court of Justice there was an increased use of chambers and a redistribution of responsibilities between it and the Court of First Instance.
- A reduction in the number of Member States required to take part in enhanced co-operation between the Member States.
- Three new competences were added to the powers of the Union:

1. the establishment of Eurojust, a unit of public prosecutors to co-ordinate the fight against crime;
2. a provision to combat fraud on the public finances; and
3. social exclusion and modernisation of social security systems was added to the objectives of social policy.

The limited achievements of Nice were insufficient to dampen calls for continued reform. At the European Council's meeting in Laeken in December 2001, it was decided to establish a Convention on the Future of Europe, with Valéry Giscard d'Estaing, a former French President as its chairperson. The Convention consisted of 113 representatives. Its main purpose was to debate the future of the Union and the adoption of a European Union Constitution, particularly:

- simplifying the treaties—reorganising the basic provisions of the present treaties into a single treaty;
- setting out the powers of the Union with particular emphasis on the principle of subsidiarity;
- considering the status of the Charter of Fundamental Rights of the European Union; and

- clarifying the role of national parliaments within the institutional structure of the Union.

In 2002, the three Communities became two, since the ECSC Treaty was designed to only last for 50 years and thus expired in July 2002. In contrast, the European Atomic Energy Community subsists beyond 2002 and exists alongside the European Union legal system. The Euro currency notes and coins were first issued on January 1, 2002.

Progress towards the European Constitution was glacial in speed. At the Brussels meeting of the European Council in December 2003, under the Italian Presidency, consensus on the form of a final document could not be achieved. Progress completely stalled in 2004, since the EU was preoccupied with its fifth and, to date, the largest ever, enlargement of the EU. This "Big Bang" expansion saw eight East European nations join (Czech Republic, Estonia, Hungary, Lithuania, Latvia, Poland, Slovakia and Slovenia), accompanied by the small island states of Malta and Cyprus. Major reforms to European competition law also came into force in 2004. Progress towards the Constitution was no better in 2005, and indeed went into reverse, when the French and Dutch populations rejected the European Constitution in national referendums, thus sounding the death knell for the Constitution.

In 2007, the sixth enlargement occurred, with Bulgaria and Romania taking the total EU membership to 27. In total, the EU now comprises a population of 501 million citizens. Institutional reform of the European Union was still urgently required, notwithstanding the rejection of the European Constitution. The radical approach to Treaty reform, exemplified by use of the inclusive and more participatory Convention approach in relation to the European Constitution project, was abandoned for the next attempt at Treaty reform in Lisbon.

The text of the Lisbon Treaty was agreed at the end of December 2007 and looked to be going the same way as the failed European Constitution, when Irish voters rejected the Lisbon Treaty in a referendum in 2008. However, a combination of the Irish voting the right way in their second Lisbon Treaty referendum in 2009, and the successful resolution of a number of national constitutional court challenges (*Wheeler* [2008]; *Decision of the Bundesverfassungsgericht* [2009]; *Decision of the Czech Constitutional Court*, November 3 [2009]) paved the way for Lisbon to come into force on December 1, 2009.

The Lisbon Treaty was designed to complete the unfinished business of both Amsterdam and Nice, by making the European Union more democratic, efficient and coherent.

The most significant elements of the Treaty of Lisbon are the following:

- Abolishment of the three pillar structure created by Maastricht. The European Union acquires legal capacity and becomes the legal successor to the European Community. The European Union is now organised according to three international treaties, namely: the Treaty on European Union; the Treaty on the Functioning of the European Union and the Charter of Fundamental Rights of the European Union; the European Union also expressly provides an exit clause for Member States wishing to leave the Union and provides for solidarity in the event of a terrorist attack or natural or man-made disaster. However, EURATOM was not brought into the EU structure.

- The number of EU institutions is increased to seven (Commission, Parliament, Council of the EU, Court of Justice of the European Union, Court of Auditors, European Council (New) and the European Central Bank (New)).
- Reform of the internal workings of the EU institutions.
- The Charter of Fundamental Rights of the European Union becomes legally binding (subject to opt-outs of the UK and Poland and the Czech Republic) and the EU is enabled to accede to the European Convention of Human Rights, through promulgation of ECHR accession directives.
- Increased democratic accountability of the EU, through: the national parliaments' increased role in supervising the application of subsidiarity; the introduction of the Citizen's Initiative, allowing 1 million EU citizens to submit legislative proposals to the European Commission; the co-decision legislative procedure becoming the default ordinary legislative procedure, providing the Parliament with an equal say in the overwhelming majority of EU legislative proposals; European Parliament becoming the joint adopter of the EU's annual budget beside the Council of the EU; and Council of the EU legislative decisions being taken in public.
- Increased coherency and consistency of EU action, through: the creation of the role of President of the European Council; the creation of the post of High Representative of the Union for Foreign Affairs and Security Policy/Vice President of the European Commission; the creation of the European External Action Service to assist the High Representative; abolition of the three pillar structure of Maastricht and clarification of the EU's powers into three categories (Exclusive, Shared and Supporting, Coordinating and Complementary action).
- Increased EU action: introduction of new EU competences such as climate change, energy, space, sport, tourism, intellectual property, civil protection, data protection, child protection, administrative cooperation, humanitarian aid and the solidarity clause; increased use of Qualified Majority Voting in the Council of the EU.

The newly reformed European Union is more structured, coherent and democratic and better prepared for a new wave of applicant States. Further enlargement of the EU will, in all likelihood, include Turkey, the Former Yugoslav Republic of Macedonia and Iceland. More immediately, Croatia became the 28th Member State of the EU on July 1, 2013. Under their agreements with the European Union, applicant countries have undertaken to fulfil stringent criteria for membership, known as the "Copenhagen Criteria". These specify that the applicant country:

- has achieved the stability of institutions guaranteeing democracy, the rule of law, respect for human rights and the protection of minorities;
- has a functioning market economy, as well as the capacity to cope with competitive pressures and forces within the union;
- has the ability to take on the obligations of membership, including the *acquis communautaire*, and be able to put into effect all EU rules and procedures. The term *acquis communautaire* refers to all principles, policies, laws, practices, obligations and objectives that have been decided and agreed upon since the establishment of the original Communities, whatever the form in which it was done, whether legally binding or not. In other words, it refers to the body of rules that govern the Union in all its fields of activity; and such activity adheres to the aims of political, economic and monetary union.

3. SOURCES OF INFORMATION

TEXTBOOKS

A.M. Dashwood, B. Rodger, M. Dougan, E. Spaventa, and D.A. *Wyatt, Wyatt & Dashwood's European Union Law*, 6th edn (London: Sweet and Maxwell, 2013).

D. Chalmers, C. Hadjiemmanuil, G. Monti and A. Tomkins, *EU Law—Text and Materials*, 2nd edn (Cambridge: CUP, 2010).

E. Szyszczak and A. Cygan, *Understanding EU Law*, 2nd edn (London: Sweet and Maxwell, 2008).

J. Fairhurst, *Law of the European Union*, 9th edn (London: Pearson, 2012).

J. Steiner and L. Woods, *Textbook on EU Law*, 11th edn (Oxford: OUP, 2013).

M. Horspool and M. Humphreys, *EU Law*, 7th edn (Oxford: OUP, 2012).

N. Foster, *Foster on EU Law*, 4th edn (Oxford: OUP, 2013).

P. Craig and G. de Burca, *EU Law—Text, Cases and Materials*, 5th edn (Oxford: OUP, 2011).

P. Kent, *Law of the European Union*, 3rd edn (Harlow: Longman, 2001).

S. Weatherill, *Cases and Materials on EC Law*, 10th edn (Oxford: OUP, 2012).

T. Kennedy, *Learning European Law* (London: Sweet and Maxwell, 1998).

STUDY SKILL TECHNIQUES

K. Fullerton, *Legal Research Skills for Scots Lawyers*, 2nd edn (Edinburgh: W. Green & Sons, 2007).

P. Clinch, *Using a Law Library* (Oxford: Blackstone Press, 2001).

S. Stein, *Law on the Web—A Guide for Students and Practitioners* (Harlow: Pearson 2003).

S.I. Strong, *How to Write Law Essays and Exams* (London: LexisNexis, 2003).

LEGISLATION—TREATIES, MAIN REGULATIONS AND DIRECTIVES, ETC.

N. Busby and R. Smith, *Core EU Legislation* (2012/2013, Palgrave Macmillan, 2012).

N. Foster, *Blackstone's EU Treaties and Legislation* (2012/2013, OUP 2013).

JUDGMENTS OF THE COURT OF JUSTICE OF THE EUROPEAN UNION

These are reproduced in the European Court Reports ("E.C.R.") and the Common Market Law Reports ("C.M.L.R.").

JOURNALS

Common Market Law Review—C.M.L.Rev.
European Competition Law Review—E.C.L.R.
European Law Review—E.L.Rev.
European Public Law—E.P.L.
Journal of Common Market Studies—J.C.M.S.

INTERNET

One of the most important sources of information is the web site of the European Union (the Europa Server)—*http://europa.eu.*

This site is the gateway to all policies, legislation and institutions of the EU. It gives multilingual access to all major issues on the EU agenda: Treaties and legislation, the Official Journal, information on the rights of European citizens, press releases from the institutions, information on the Euro (€), up-to-date information on decisions, programmes or measures adopted by the EU, publications and statistics, the nearest available sources of information and case law from the European Courts of Justice.

What's New on Europa
http://europa.eu/geninfo/whatsnew.htm

RAPID: EU Press Releases
http://europa.eu/press_room/index_en.htm

EUR-Lex, access to full-text legislative information including Treaties, legislation, case law and the Official Journal.
http://eur-lex.europa.eu/

European Parliament
http://www.europarl.europa.eu/

Council of the EU
http://www.consilium.europa.eu/

The European Council
http://www.european-council.europa.eu/

European Commission
http://ec.europa.eu/

Court of Justice
http://www.curia.europa.eu/

Court of Auditors
http://www.eca.europa.eu/

European Economic and Social Committee
http://www.eesc.europa.eu/

Committee of the Regions
http://www.cor.europa.eu/

European Central Bank
http://www.ecb.int/

KEEPING UP TO DATE

BBC Europe
http://news.bbc.co.uk/1/hi/world/europe/default.stm

BBC Europe Today
http://www.bbc.co.uk/worldservice/programmes/europetoday/index.shtml

EU Business website
http://www.eubusiness.com/

EurActiv
http://www.euractiv.com/en/

4. SOURCES OF LAW

The founding Treaties do not define the sources of European Union Law. Article 19 of the Treaty of European Union ("TEU") simply provides that the Court of Justice shall ensure that in the interpretation and application of the Treaties the law is observed. However, reflecting the diversity and supranational nature of the European Union legal system, the sources of law can be classified into the following four main sources.

(1) TREATIES

The two European Union Treaties (and their accompanying Protocols and Annexes by virtue of art.51 TEU)) and the *Charter of Fundamental Rights of the European Union* are the primary sources of Union law and its ultimate legal authority:

- Treaty on European Union;
- Treaty on the Functioning of the European Union ("TFEU"); and
- The Charter of Fundamental Rights of the European Union.

In addition, the *European Atomic Energy Community Treaty 1957* ("Euratom") is still in force, notwithstanding the changes wrought by the Treaty of Lisbon.

Other treaties made between Member States including those amending the founding treaties and accession treaties of new Member States:

- Merger Treaty 1965;
- Budgetary Treaties 1970, 1975;
- Single European Act 1986;
- Treaty on European Union 1992 (the Maastricht Treaty);
- Treaty of Amsterdam 1997;
- Treaty of Nice 2000;
- Treaty of Lisbon 2007 and
- The various Treaties of Accession.

Treaties between the Union and non-Member States:

- Treaty establishing the World Trade Organisation;
- The Cotonou Agreement (Consolidated version June 2010) between the EU and the African, Caribbean and Pacific ("ACP") countries; and
- Europe Agreements between the European Union and applicant countries for membership of the European Union.

(2) SECONDARY LEGISLATION

This refers to the body of Union rules adopted in accordance with the founding Treaties. It has evolved over the years from the 100 articles of the ECSC Treaty, into a vast body of law comprising thousands of regulations, directives, decisions, agreements and other measures. These are the binding and non-binding Acts of the institutions. Each institution must act within the limits of the powers conferred upon it by art.288 TFEU which states:

> "To exercise the Union's competences, the institutions shall adopt regulations, directives, decisions, recommendations and opinions.
>
> A regulation shall have general application. It shall be binding in its entirety and directly applicable in all Member States.
>
> A directive shall be binding, as to the result to be achieved, upon each Member State to which it is addressed, but shall leave to the national authorities the choice of form and methods.
>
> A decision shall be binding in its entirety upon those to whom it is addressed.
>
> Recommendations and opinions shall have no binding force."

Article 288 TFEU therefore sets out three types of legally binding acts:

- Regulations;
- Directives; and
- Decisions.

And two types of non-legally binding acts:

- Recommendations (art.292 TFEU); and
- Opinions.

Confusingly, the Treaty on the Functioning of the European Union also provides that regulations, directives and decisions can be non-legislative in nature and, further, may be categorised as delegated and implementing acts (arts 290, 291 and 297(2) TFEU).

Legislation must have a legal basis

Whichever form of legislation is chosen, it fulfils a specific function in the development of Union law and therefore the treaties specify which type of act must be adopted to achieve a particular aim of the Union. The preamble to any piece of legislation should therefore state the Article of the Treaties on which it is based. The chosen Treaty Article will set out the legislative procedure to be followed—involving voting requirements in the Council and the extent of the European Parliament's involvement in the process.

Article 296 TFEU sets out that legal acts must state the reasons on which they are based and must refer to relevant proposals, initiatives, recommendations, requests and opinions which were required by the treaties. The institution concerned is not allowed to specify how it would *prefer* the objective to be pursued. Its conviction must be based on objective factors, which must be amenable to judicial review. In particular, these factors must include the aim and content of the measure (*Commission v Council Re Titanium Dioxide Waste* [1991]; *Commission v Council "Environmental Crimes"* [2005]; *Commission v Parliament and Council (Shipments of Waste)* [2009]; and *Parliament v Council (Energy Infrastructure projects)* [2012]). The measure must therefore specify in a clear and concise manner what the principal issues of fact and law are so that the reasoning which led the institution to make its choice of legal basis may be clearly understood. If an act of an institution is not sufficiently reasoned, this constitutes a ground for annulment of the measure (see Ch.7, Judicial Review).

The full citation convention for secondary legislation is as follows:

- form of legislation (regulation, directive, etc.);
- number of the instrument and its year of adoption (regulations are cited by number then year, directives and decisions by year then number);
- treaty from which authority for the legislation is founded;
- the institution adopting the legislation (Commission, Council);
- date passed;
- title; and
- date and page number of the Official Journal in which the measure was published.

For example—Council Directive 2013/1/EU of December 20, 2012 amending Directive 93/109/EC as regards certain detailed arrangements for the exercise of the right to stand as a candidate in elections to the European Parliament for citizens of the Union residing in a Member State of which they are not nationals ([2013] O.J. L 26/27).

Regulations

"A regulation shall have general application. It shall be binding in its entirety and directly applicable in all Member States."

- "General application" means that a regulation applies to any number of Member States, individuals or companies.
- "Binding in its entirety" means that the whole of the regulation must be implemented.
- "Directly applicable" means that the regulation applies in all Member States without the need for further enactment, that is the Regulation is self-executing. Member States are thus precluded from giving effect to the terms of a Regulation through enactment of domestic provisions, although administrative measures designed to facilitate the objectives of the Regulation are permissible (*Leonesio*

[1972]; *Commission v Italy (The Slaughtered Cow)* [1973]; *Commission v UK (Tachographs)* [1973]; *Handlbauer* [2004]; *Horvath* [2009]; and *Rakvere Piim* [2011]).

● "In all Member States" means that the regulation must be applied in the same way and at the same time in all Member States.
● Regulations must be published in the Official Journal in the 23 official Union languages. They enter into force on the date specified in the act, or if no date is specified, then on the 20th day following their publication.

Directives

"A Directive shall be binding, as to the result to be achieved, upon each Member State to which it is addressed, but shall leave it to the national authorities the choice of form and methods."

● The purpose of directives is to allow the achievement of common objectives throughout the Member States.
● Directives are addressed to Member States only.
● The Member State must enact domestic legislation to comply with the directive within a set time limit.
● The form of the implementing legislation is chosen by the Member State which can choose the most appropriate method for its own legal system. (This autonomy extends to allowing differentiated transposition of EU law obligations within devolved regions of a Member State (*Horvath* [2009]).)
● Once they have been correctly transposed into national law, obligations derived from directives are binding on individuals through that national law.
● Individuals may claim compensation if a Member State fails to implement a directive within the time limit or does so incompletely or incorrectly.
● Directives must be published in the Official Journal in the 23 official Union languages.

Decisions

"A decision shall be binding in its entirety upon those to whom it is addressed."

● "Binding in its entirety" means that the whole of the decision must be implemented.
● A decision is binding only upon those to whom it is addressed.
● A decision can be addressed to a Member State or to an individual or company.
● There is no need to enact implementing legislation.
● Decisions must be notified to those to whom they are addressed and do not come into effect until that notification has been carried out.
● Decisions can be challenged before the Court of Justice by persons

who claim to be directly and individually affected; and
- Decisions affecting the rights of third parties are published in the Official Journal in the 23 official Union languages.

Recommendations and opinions

"Recommendations and opinions shall have no binding force." They are of persuasive force only (*Grimaldi* [1989]).

(3) CASE LAW OF THE COURT OF JUSTICE OF THE EUROPEAN UNION

The decisions of the Court of Justice of the European Union are authoritative on all aspects of the Treaties, acts of the institutions and acts of the Member States which arise in conformity with their obligations under the Treaties. Unlike the common law tradition of Anglo-American systems, the civilian nature of Union law based on continental legal systems does not rely on the doctrine of precedent and means that the Court of Justice is not rigidly bound by its own previous decisions, although the principle of legal certainty means that in practice the Court does follow its earlier rulings. Nevertheless, the Court may depart from them if it feels the need to adapt or update its case law (Keck and Mithouard [1993]).

(4) GENERAL PRINCIPLES OF LAW

As well as the Treaties, the Court of Justice draws on general principles of law derived from the legal traditions of the Member States. These general principles can be used by all courts to interpret Union law and have constitutional status within the EU legal system. They are generally recognised as comprising:

- proportionality—legislative measures should not go beyond what is necessary to achieve the desired objective (*Bela-Mühle v Grows Farm* [1977]; *Müller Fleisch* [2010]);
- equal treatment/non-discrimination—(*Marks and Spencer* [2008]; *Navas* [2006]; *Assurances de Credit v Council and Commission* [1991]). It includes provisions as to age (*Mangold* [2006]; *Kücükdeveci* [2010] and arts 20 and 21 of the Charter of Fundamental Rights);
- legal certainty—comprising respect for legitimate expectations and the principle that European Union measures should not have retroactive effect (*Council v European Parliament* [1986]; *Förster* [2008]);
- legitimate expectations (*Mulder v Minister van Landbouw en Visserij* [1988]; *Spain v Council* [2006]);

- legal professional privilege—written communication between independent (not in-house) lawyers and clients are respected (*AM & S Europe Ltd v Commission* [1982] and *Akzo Nobel* [2010]);
- the right to property (*Raffinerie Mediterranee* [2010]; art.17 of the Charter of Fundamental Rights)
- the right to pursue an economic activity (*Arcelor* [2010]; art.16 of the Charter of Fundamental Rights) (including the right of contractual freedom (*Opinion of Advocate General Kokott in Commission v Alrosa* [2009]));
- fundamental human rights—in *Nold v Commission* [1974] the Court stated that while it was inspired by the constitutional traditions common to the Member States, it added "international treaties for the protection of human rights", which was clearly a reference to the European Convention for the Protection of Human Rights and Fundamental Freedoms (*Kadi and Al Barakaat* [2008]).

Further, the Charter of Fundamental Rights will increasingly be relied on by the Court of Justice, to justify EU action.

5. INSTITUTIONS

The nature of the EU institutions is unique not only in their structure but in the way they interact in the performance of the legislative, executive and judicial functions of the Union.

By virtue of the Lisbon Treaty there are seven main institutions serving the European Union (art.13 TEU). They are:

- the European Commission which acts in the interests of the Union;
- the Council of the European Union (formerly known as the Council of Ministers) representing the Member States;
- the European Council, comprising the Heads of State or Government of the Member States and designed to provide the Union with political impetus (added by virtue of the Treaty of Lisbon);
- the European Parliament representing the peoples of Europe;
- the Court of Justice of the European Union;
- the European Court of Auditors which oversees the probity of the Union's budget (became an institution by virtue of the Maastricht Treaty); and
- the European Central Bank, which administers and oversees the smooth running of the Euro (€) currency—to date, 17 member States have adopted the Euro as their currency. (The ECB became an EU institution by virtue of the Treaty of Lisbon.)

What distinguishes an institution from any other Union body is that an institution may take binding decisions and that their members are either elected nationally (as in the case of the Council and the European Parliament) or appointed by the governments of the Member States or by the Council. Other bodies, such as the Committee of the Regions, either play a purely consultative role or take decisions which are not binding.

A number of other bodies have been created to assist and advise the institutions. These include:

- the Economic and Social Committee—an advisory committee comprised of representatives of various economic and social groups such as "producers, farmers, carriers, workers, dealers, craftsmen, professional occupations, consumers and the general public". Currently there are 353 members (arts 300 to 304 TFEU);
- the Committee of the Regions—a consultative committee of local and regional authorities holding an electoral mandate to represent citizens at a local level. Currently there are 353 members. The committee advises on matters of particular concern to European regions. In particular, the Treaty provides for it to be consulted in the

areas of culture, public health, economic and social cohesion and environmental policy (arts 300 and 305 to 307 TFEU);
- the European Investment Bank—set up to manage the Structural Fund and other Union funds on a non-profit-making basis to aid the less developed regions and to assist in funding projects affecting more than one Member State where they cannot be funded sufficiently from within those Member States themselves (arts 308 to 309 TFEU); and
- the European System of Central Banks. The European System of Central Banks is the umbrella term for the economic coordination and cooperation which takes place between the European Central Bank and the National Central Banks ("NCB") of the Member States, including the national banks of Member States that have yet to adopt the Euro.

THE EUROPEAN COMMISSION

Composition

The Commission is composed of 28 commissioners, one for each Member State. The Treaty of Nice stated that if and when the Union consisted of 27 Member States, the number of commissioners would have to be less than the number of Member States, with the exact number and nationality to be agreed by the Council of Ministers acting unanimously and based on the principles of equality, demography and geography. Subsequently, the failure to ratify the European Constitution and the enlargement of the EU created a situation whereby the Council simply decided to continue with the present system of one Commission member for each Member State until 2009. The Lisbon Treaty continues the principle of one commissioner per Member State for the Commission appointed for the term 2010–2014 (The Barroso II Commission) (art.17(4) TEU). Beyond 2014, the Commission shall comprise a number of commissioners equating to 2/3 thirds the number of Member States, unless the European Council decides, by unanimity, to change this numbering (art.17(5) TEU).

The method by which the Commission is appointed is that the European Council nominates the President of the Commission by qualified majority. The European Parliament then approves the candidate by majority vote. (In the event of the Parliament not agreeing to the candidacy, the European Council would have to nominate a new candidate.) The President-Elect so approved, in conjunction with the Council, then produces a list of Commissioners-nominate. The entire Commission so constituted must then gain the consent of the European Parliament. The Parliament may not choose which of the Commissioners it likes (or dislikes). Approval is by a vote of confidence en bloc, although political pressure may be applied by the Parliament prior to the vote, in order to force a new commissioner-designate to be included in the list of commissioners going forward. The

European Council then approves the entire Commission, by qualified majority (art.17(7) TEU).

The commissioners serve for a renewable five-year term and are chosen on grounds of their general competence, their commitment to the European Union and "whose independence is beyond doubt".

The Commission is subject to other supervision by the Parliament, as follows:

- Parliament may censure the entire Commission.
- Parliament must receive monthly reports from the Commission on the implementation of the budget.
- Parliament must be presented with the Commission's Annual General Report.

To ensure their independence commissioners are forbidden to seek or take instructions from any government or other body and must refrain from any action which is not compatible with their duties (Commissioner Dalli resigned in October 2012). All the Member States have accepted this principle and no influence is brought to bear upon the Commissioners in the performance of their tasks. Their duties are solely to further the wider interests of the Union. During their term of office, commissioners may not engage in any other occupation and even after they retire, they are bound to behave with integrity and discretion as regards the acceptance of certain appointments or benefits.

A commissioner will be forced to resign if the President requests such resignation (art.17(6) TEU). Under an inter-institutional Framework Agreement between the Parliament and the Commission from February 2010, the Parliament has the right to ask the Commission President to ask for the resignation of an individual commissioner. Commissioners may also be compulsorily retired by the Court of Justice of the European Union, where the commissioner is either found guilty of serious misconduct or no longer fulfils the criteria for being a commissioner (art.247 TFEU).

As well as allowing commissioners to fulfil their tasks with complete impartiality, the collegiate nature of the Commission also protects them from undue pressure. Commissioners do not fulfil individual roles under the Treaties, except for the President and the Vice President who is also the High Representative for Foreign Affairs and Security Policy (arts 16(6) and 18(4) TEU) (Catherine Ashton was appointed the first High Representative). Decisions are thus made by simple majority, dissenting opinions are not published and all members of the college of commissioners bear collective responsibility on the political level for all decisions adopted.

Functions and Powers

The administrative responsibility of the Commission is divided up into 33 Directorates-General ("D-G"), at least one of which is allocated by the President to the portfolio of an individual commissioner. They cover such specific areas of responsibility such as external relations, competition, and so on. Two new D-Gs were created by virtue of the Lisbon Treaty, namely energy and climate action. Each commissioner is assisted by a cabinet headed by a Chef de Cabinet. There are also specialised services such as the Legal Service, which advises the Directorates-General and represent the Commission in legal proceedings, and the Statistical and Publications Office. In total there are over 40 D-Gs and specialist service departments in the Commission. The total staff of the Commission is approximately 34,000 and comprises administrative and secretarial support staff, experts, translators and interpreters.

The Commission's powers and functions are laid down in the Treaty under arts 244 to 250 TFEU. They fall into three main categories.

(1) *Guardian of the Treaties*
The Commission has been given the power to ensure that the provisions of the Treaty and the measures adopted for their implementation are applied (art.17 TEU).

It monitors the performance of the Member States in complying with their obligations under the Treaties and may receive complaints from individuals or companies who believe that a Member State is infringing their Union rights. Under art.258 TFEU proceedings, the Commission may investigate and prosecute Member States alleged to be in breach of their Treaty obligations (*Commission v United Kingdom (Equal Treatment)* [2010]; *Commission v France (Money Laundering and Terrorist Financing* [2010]; *Commission v Spain (Emergency Plans)* [2010]; and *Commission v France (Railways)* [2013]; *Commission v United Kingdom (Taxation)* [2013]). This general enforcement power will be extended to cover pre-existing Treaty obligations concerning police and judicial cooperation in criminal matters, once five years have elapsed from the entry into force of the Lisbon Treaty (art.10 of Protocol 36).

These obligations (sometimes known as "the loyalty clause" of the Treaty) are set out in art.4.3 TEU which states that:

> "Member States shall take any appropriate measures, general or particular, to ensure fulfilment of the obligations arising out of the Treaties or resulting from the acts of the institutions of the Union. The member States shall facilitate the achievement of the Union's tasks and refrain from any measure which could jeopardise the attainment of the Union's objectives."

When the Commission considers that a Member State has not fulfilled an obligation under Union law, it takes the following steps:

- It reminds the government in question of its obligations and invites it to take the necessary measures or submit its observations, all within a time limit set by the Commission, normally two months.
- If no action is taken by the Member State and no observations are received, or if those that were submitted do not convince the

Commission, it delivers a "reasoned opinion" on the matter and lays down a time limit within which the Member State must comply.

- If the Member State does not comply, the Commission may bring the matter before the Court of Justice.
- If the Court finds that the Member State has indeed failed to fulfil its obligation, "the State shall be required to take the necessary steps to comply with the judgment".

The procedure for enforcing Member States' fulfilment of their Union obligations is therefore in two stages. The first is an informal stage during which the Commission issues the formal notice and eventually a reasoned opinion to the Member State. In practice though, the Commission endeavours to negotiate a settlement. The second stage is the formal judicial stage where the Commission refers the Member State to the Court of Justice.

There is also a right for a Member State to take action against another Member State under art.259 TFEU for failure to fulfil its Union obligations. The procedure requires that the matter be brought to the attention of the Commission. Proceedings then mirror those under art.258 TFEU, with the added requirement that the Commission requests the observations of *both* Member States involved. Actions brought under this heading are extremely rare as this procedure tends to be politically contentious. To date, only four cases have reached the Court: *France v UK* [1979]; *Belgium v Spain* [2000]; *Spain v UK* [2007]; and *Hungary v Slovakia* [2012].

In order to promote compliance with Treaty obligations, art.260 TFEU provides that in cases where the Member State has not taken the necessary steps to comply with the judgment of the Court, the Commission shall, after giving the Member State the opportunity to submit its observations, issue a reasoned opinion specifying the points on which the Member State has not complied and fixing a time limit for this to be carried out. In case of non-compliance, the Commission may bring the matter again to the Court and specify the amount of the lump sum or penalty payment to be paid. If the Court finds that the Member State has indeed not complied with its judgment, it may impose a lump sum or penalty payment (*Commission v Greece* [2000]; [2009]; and *Commission v Ireland* [2012]). As well as the penalties provided for in the Treaties to encourage Member States to fulfil their Union obligations, pecuniary sanctions can also be imposed on Member States where they breach Union law to the detriment of an individual (see Member State Liability).

The Commission also monitors the acts of the EU's institutions, where such acts are intended to produce legal effects vis-à-vis third parties, and may initiate an action against them when it is believed that:

- their failure to act constitutes an infringement of the Treaties (art.265 TFEU); or
- an act of the institution constitutes an infringement of the Treaty (art.263 TFEU).

(2) *Initiator of Union Action*

The Commission has historically had the right of legislative initiative in that it is empowered to propose legislation for its adoption by the Council and the European Parliament acting in accordance with the Union's legislative procedures. Legislation must encompass three core objectives. First, the Commission must identify the European interest; second, it must organise consultation as widely as necessary; and third, it must respect the principle of subsidiarity (see Ch.6, European Law and National Law). In fulfilment of this task, the Commission works closely with the Union's two consultative bodies, the Economic and Social Committee and the Committee of the Regions, and consults them on most items of draft legislation.

The Treaty on European Union allows the Council and Parliament to request that the Commission submit appropriate proposals for legislation where these are required for the purpose of implementing the Treaty. Further, the Treaty of Lisbon allows for European citizens to submit legislative proposals to the Commission, by virtue of the Citizens' Initiative as set out in art.11(4) TEU and Regulation 211/2011. The regulation provided for the system to become fully operational as of April 1, 2012.

The Commission will then issue preparatory documents, such as Green Papers containing a description of a problem and its proposal for solving it; this will be followed by a White Paper outlining the proposed legislation for consultation. The general principle of transparency that the public should have the widest possible access to documents held by the Commission, the Parliament and the Council—subject to public interest or the rights of privacy of the individual—has been adopted through Regulation 1049/2001 which sets out that refusal to grant access must be based on one of the exceptions provided for within the regulation and must be justified on the grounds that disclosure of the document in question would be harmful.

The Commission's significant role in shaping the Union's priorities has increased in importance over recent years—for example in preparing for the final completion of the single market and for enlargement of the Union in the 21st century.

(3) *Executive of the Union*

The Commission has been given its own power of decision which it exercises in the functioning and development of the internal market, for example in furtherance of the Union's competition policy where it administers and enforces the competition rules, and regulates mergers, joint ventures and acquisitions.

It also administers the customs union, the common agricultural policy, state aids and the common commercial policy. Although the majority of European policies are administered by the Member States themselves, the Commission has significant supervisory powers. In this connection it may make regulations which must be observed within the Member States and ensures that these regulations are carried out.

A significant part of its executive function is to manage the Union budget for submission to the Council and administer special funds, such as the European Agricultural Guarantee Fund, the European Regional Development Fund, the Cohesion Fund and the European Social Fund, which all form part of the budget.

The Commission also acts as negotiator of international trade and co-operation agreements with third countries, or groups of countries, which the Council then concludes.

The Commission used to also act by way of a delegated legislative power from the Council, known as "Comitology". This practice of decision-making involved the Commission's legislative activities being supervised by the Council under a complex system involving the submission of the Commission's draft implementing measures to committees composed of officials from Member States. "Comitology" was subject to a range of cogent criticisms so the Lisbon Treaty has provided for a new delegated power for the Commission under arts 290 and 291 TFEU. Under these new procedures, legislative acts of the Council and the Parliament can provide that the Commission be able to supplement or amend that legislation and, in the case of implementing acts of the Member States, the Commission is given an executive power to create uniform implementing conditions for these national acts.

The European institutional structure is not characterised by a rigid separation of powers. The Commission, for example, plays a role that is legislative, executive, judicial and administrative. It is:

- the guardian of the Treaties;
- initiator and co-ordinator of Union policy; and
- the executive agency of the Union.

COUNCIL OF THE EUROPEAN UNION ("THE COUNCIL")

The Council of the European Union—referred to previously as the Council of Ministers—is a body with the characteristics of both a supranational and an intergovernmental organisation. It is composed of representatives from the Member States at ministerial level, authorised to commit the government of that Member State. In practice this means that its membership fluctuates depending on the subject under discussion. For example, the General Affairs Council deals with institutional and policy issues whilst the Foreign Affairs Council deals with external issues and is chaired by the High Representative for Foreign Affairs and Security Policy. Both of these configurations will be attended by national Foreign Ministers. Ministers for Agriculture, Transport, Finance, etc., constitute the membership of the Council when it discusses policy and legislation in those areas. In total, there are 10 different Council configurations, but in legal terms there is only one Council of the EU.

The Council is assisted in its work by COREPER I and II (The

Committees of Permanent Representatives) consisting of senior national ambassadors and their deputies who are permanently located in Brussels (art.240 TFEU). The work of these Committees allow decisions to be made by the Council by examining Commission proposals and preparing items for discussion at Council meetings (art.16(7) TEU). COREPER is assisted by a wide range of specialist advisory committees and working parties.

The Council's powers and functions are laid down in art.237 to art.243 TFEU. The Council:

- is the European Union's main decision-making institution and final legislative authority exercising power for the whole spectrum of the Union's activities;
- the Treaty of Lisbon strengthened the role of the European Parliament and now the Council's budgetary and legislative powers are shared jointly with the Parliament (art.16(1) TEU);
- depending on the subject under discussion and the voting procedures specified in the Treaties, acts by a simple majority of its members, by a qualified majority or by unanimous decision. Where the Council acts by a qualified majority, the votes of each of its members, until October 2014, are weighted as follows (Protocol 9 of the Treaty of Lisbon):

Country	Votes	Country	Votes
Austria	10	Latvia	4
Belgium	12	Lithuania	7
Bulgaria	10	Luxembourg	4
Croatia	7	Malta	3
Cyprus	4	Netherlands	13
Czech Republic	12	Poland	27
Denmark	7	Portugal	12
Estonia	4	Romania	14
Finland	7	Spain	27
France	29	Slovakia	7
Germany	29	Slovenia	4
Greece	12	Sweden	10
Hungary	12	United Kingdom	29
Ireland	7		
Italy	29	**TOTAL**	**352**

First, there must be at least 260 votes in favour. Thus, 93 negative votes mean that the measure will not come into force. Second, a majority of the Member States must be in favour of the measure. In some cases the Treaties may require a two-thirds majority. Third, a Member State can request verification that the qualified majority comprises at least 62 per cent of the total population of the Union before the act may be adopted. The Lisbon Treaty provides that after 2014, the voting scheme will be amended and simplified such that, in most cases, a qualified majority would be calculated as being 55 per cent of the Member States in favour, which would be at least 15 in number, representing 65 per cent of the Union's population, with four large member States being able to block a legislative proposal. In specific cases where the Council is not acting on a proposal from the Commission or the High Representative for Foreign Affairs, then QMV would be defined as 72 per cent of the member States, representing 65 per cent of the EU's population (arts 16(4) TEU and 238(2) TFEU).

Legislation takes the form of regulations, directives, decisions, recommendations and opinions (see Ch.4, Sources of Law).

The Council may also adopt conclusions of a political nature or other types of acts, such as common positions, declarations or resolutions. Furthermore, the Council establishes requirements for the Commission to exercise the implementing powers conferred upon it.

Democratic accountability of the Council was significantly enhanced by the Treaty of Lisbon amendments that require the Council to meet in public when deliberating and voting upon legislative proposals (art.16(8) TEU). Further, greater transparency has been achieved through allowing enhanced access to Council, Commission and European Parliament documents, subject to limits on the grounds of public and private interest (see above, under "The Commission").

European Union legislation, as well as the Council's common positions forwarded to the European Parliament, are published in the Official Journal in all 24 official languages.

The Council also:

- co-ordinates the general economic policies of the Member States (subject to the principle of subsidiarity) (art.5 TFEU);
- concludes international agreements on behalf of the European Union (which are negotiated by the Commission and require, in some cases, Parliament's consultation or consent) between the Union and a state, a group of states or international organisations (Pt 5 TFEU);
- in conjunction with the European Parliament, adopts the Union budget after its preparation by the Commission (art.314 TFEU);
- takes the decisions necessary to define and implement the Common Foreign and Security Policy (art.26(2) TEU); and
- adopts measures, regulations and directives and takes decisions in the Area of Freedom, Security and Justice (Title V TFEU).

The Presidency of the Council is held by each Member State on a six-monthly rotating basis and plays a vital part as the driving force in the legislative and political decision-making process. It organises and chairs all meetings and works out compromises to resolve difficulties.

THE EUROPEAN PARLIAMENT

Composition
The European Parliament presently consists of 766 members representing 507 million citizens in the 28 Member States of the European Union, with a minimum number of MEPS from one Member State being fixed at six and the maximum number being 96. Since 1979 the Parliament has been directly elected every five years throughout all the Member States. The previous Treaty of Nice provided that the maximum number of MEPs be fixed at 736, however the maximum number of MEPs was raised by Lisbon to 751 (art.14(2) TEU and Protocol 36). The European Parliamentary elections of June 2009 were held under the old Treaty of Nice rules. As a consequence of Lisbon coming into force, 12 Member States gained a number of additional MEPs, whilst Germany should have lost three MEPs, but, by EU law, MEPs holding a mandate cannot be deprived of their position during a parliamentary term. Therefore, the net result was that 18 MEPs joined the Parliament for the parliamentary term 2009–2014, which took the total number of MEPs to 754, exceeding the limit set out in the Lisbon Treaty and thus requiring a Treaty change, agreed by all the Member States in December 2011. Further, when Croatia acceded to the European Union, 12 new MEPs were appointed.

Citizens of the European Union are eligible to vote and stand for election (art.22 TFEU and art.39 of the Charter of Fundamental Rights).

From December 2011, the allocation of seats is as follows:

Country	Seats
Cyprus, Estonia, Luxembourg, Malta	6
Slovenia	8
Latvia	9
Croatia, Ireland, Lithuania	12
Denmark, Finland, Slovakia	13
Bulgaria	18
Austria	19
Sweden	20
Belgium, Czech Republic, Greece, Hungary, Portugal	22
Netherlands	26
Romania	33
Poland	51
Spain	54
Italy, United Kingdom	73 (The UK figure includes 6 representatives from Scotland)
France	74
Germany	99
TOTAL	**766**

MEPs sit in seven political groups rather than in national delegations. Although its committee meetings generally take place in Brussels, it meets in plenary sitting at Strasbourg for one week a month. Parliament's secretariat is located in Luxembourg. During its sessions, simultaneous translation of its debates is provided and all documentation is translated and published in the Official Journal in the official Union languages. It elects its own president and 14 vice-presidents who together form "the Bureau"—the executive body which drafts agendas, decides on matters of competence and makes the preliminary draft of Parliament's budget. The Parliament also has 20 committees.

As well as exercising its three main functions (below), Parliament takes an active part in Europe's political life by commissioning reports and passing resolutions on issues of a social and political nature such as concern for human rights. It has also contributed in no small measure to the establishment of a European Veterinary Agency in Dublin and the creation of the European Anti-Fraud Office for budgetary matters.

Functions and Powers
The functions and powers of Parliament are laid out in arts 223–234 TFEU. They fall into three main categories:

- Supervisory;
- Legislative; and
- Budgetary

Supervisory
Parliament has general supervisory powers over the other institutions of which the most powerful is its ability to hold the Commission accountable for its activities.

At the request of a quarter of its members, Parliament may, under art.226 TFEU, set up temporary Committees of Inquiry to investigate alleged contraventions or maladministration in the implementation of European law, and to appoint a Parliamentary Ombudsman under art.228 TFEU to investigate complaints such as discrimination, refusal of information or needless delays on the part of other institutions (except for the Court of Justice of the European Union).

It may receive petitions from individuals or companies in the Member States on any matter within the Union's fields of activities.

Members of the European Parliament can put written or oral questions to the Commission and to the Council or make recommendations.

The appointment of the Commission, its President and the High Representative for Foreign Affairs by the Council, is dependent upon the Parliament's consent. In general, the Commission is responsible to the European Parliament and the Parliament may require the Commission to resign in the event of a motion of censure being carried.

Legislative

Originally, the Treaty of Rome allowed the European Parliament to act only in a consultative capacity. Successive Treaty amendments have extended this purely advisory role to one which fully involves Parliament in the legislative process. Under the Lisbon Treaty, the power to make legislation is now shared jointly by the Council and Parliament (art.14(1) TEU). The extent to which this is exercised is specified within the Treaties depending on the nature of the provision authorising action by the Union for a particular purpose (the legal basis).

Normally, legislation is enacted according to the ordinary legislative procedure, as set out in art.294 TFEU (art.289 TFEU).

Under this procedure, the Commission will submit a legislative proposal to the Parliament and the Council. Parliament shares the decision-making power equally with the Council. A legal act is adopted if Council and Parliament agree at first reading. If they disagree, a second reading is required. At this stage if no agreement is forthcoming, a "conciliation committee" composed of equal numbers of MEPs and members of the Council, with the Commission present, endeavours to find a compromise on which both the Council and Parliament can subsequently agree. Ultimately, the legislative text may be adopted at third reading. If no agreement is reached, the proposed act is deemed not to have been adopted.

In addition to the ordinary legislative procedure, the Treaty on the Functioning of the European Union provides for a range of special legislative procedures (art.289 TFEU). Depending upon the nature of the laws to be adopted, special legislative procedures may either require that the Parliament simply be consulted on the measure or that the consent of the Parliament is required.

The most significant areas of EU action, in which the Parliament must give its consent, are as follows:

- determination that a Member State is at risk of seriously breaching the EU's values (art.7 TEU);
- the power to take action to combat certain forms of discrimination (art.19 TFEU);
- amendment of the scope of EU citizenship rights under art.20(2) TFEU (art.25 TFEU)
- the accession of new Member States (art.49 TEU);
- arrangements for the withdrawal of a Member State from the EU (art.50 TEU);
- the conclusion of certain international agreements (art.218 TFEU) such as association agreements and European Union accession to the European Convention on Human Rights (art.6(2) TEU);
- enhanced cooperation measures under art.20(2) TEU (art.329 TFEU) (an example of which is Regulation 1257/2012 on unitary patent protection); and
- exercise of the general power to take action (art.352 TEU).

Budgetary

The European Parliament, through a special legislative procedure, is jointly involved with the Council in establishing the budget (art.314 TFEU). If agreement cannot be reached on the budget at the start of the financial year, the Union moves onto an emergency monthly budget system, based on 1/12th of last year's budget (art.315 TFEU).

THE COURT OF JUSTICE OF THE EUROPEAN UNION

The origins of the Court of Justice of the European Union ("CJEU") can be traced to the founding Treaties (ECSC, Euratom and the EEC) which established a Court of Justice for each community. These were then merged into one single Court of Justice for the European Communities. The Single European Act created a Court of First Instance to reduce the workload of the Court. It began sitting in 1989, with limited jurisdiction—staff cases, competition and anti-dumping cases and some matters relating to the ECSC and Euratom.

After the Treaty of Lisbon, the European Court of Justice is now subdivided into three configurations, namely the Court of Justice, the General Court (formerly the Court of First Instance) and the Civil Service Tribunal (art.19 TEU). The Civil Service Tribunal is an example of the use of the power under the Functioning Treaty to create specialised court configurations. The Court of Justice of the European Union is based in Luxembourg and should not be confused with the European Court of Human Rights which has its home in Strasbourg and is *not* an institution for the European Union. It is the role of the Court of Justice to be the guardian of European Union law in accordance with art.19 TEU which states simply that, "the Court of Justice ... shall ensure that in the interpretation and application of the Treaties the law is observed".

The law referred to consists of the Treaties, secondary legislation (such as regulations, directives and decisions) and the case law of the Court itself.

The Court of Justice

Composition

The Court consists of 28 judges, one from each Member State (art.19(2) TEU). It may sit in plenary session as a full court (*Commission v Cresson* [2006]; and *Pringle v Ireland* [2012]), as a Grand Chamber consisting of 15 judges (*TNT Express Nederland* [2010]; *Gbagbo v Council* [2013]), or in chambers of three or five judges. Certain legal actions may require the Court to sit as a full Court, however the Court also has the right to decide to sit as a full court of its own motion (art.16 of the Statute of the CJEU). Member States or Union institutions party to legal proceedings may request that the court convene as a Grand Chamber and the Court also has the discretion to sit as a Grand Chamber of its own motion. Its deliberations take place in private and result in a single, collegiate judgment. The working language of the Court is French, though documents are translated into all official languages of the Union.

The Court is assisted by eight Advocates-General whose task is to examine the cases and deliver reasoned opinions to the Court. In the future, the number of Advocates-General may rise to 11, with Poland gaining a permanent Advocate-General (Declaration 38 of the Treaty of Lisbon). Both judges and Advocates-General are appointed for a period of six years. The President of the Court is elected every three years by its judges, and 14 and 13 of the judges are replaced every three years alternately. Presidents of the five-strong chambers preside for three years, whilst the Presidents of the three-strong chambers only preside for a year. All of the judges are chosen from those:

> "[W]hose independence is beyond doubt and who possess the qualifications required for appointment to the highest judicial offices in their respective countries or who are jurisconsults of recognised competence." (art.253 TFEU)

The judges are appointed by a two stage process. First, a panel of seven legal experts, who are either ex-CJEU judges, domestic supreme court justices or recognised legal experts, give their opinion on the suitability of the judges-nominate. Upon receipt of this report, the judges-nominate are then appointed by common accord of the governments of the Member States. Each Member State has a judge on the Court to represent the legal tradition of that particular country rather than the Member State itself. The Court is also assisted by a Registrar, Legal Secretaries and two Directorates.

Functions and Powers

The Court's functions and powers are set out in art.19 TEU and arts 251–281 TFEU, as well as within its own Rules of Procedure (most recently amended in September 2012: [2012] O.J. L 265/1).

The Court's jurisdiction comprises the following areas:

(1) Infringement actions against Member States, particularly—
    (a) Commission v Member States (art.258 TFEU);
    (b) Member State v Member State (art.259 TFEU);
    (c) Member State's failure to fulfil a Treaty obligation (art.260 TFEU).

(2) The legality of Union action or inaction (arts 263 and 265 TFEU), subject to certain exceptions whereby the General Court exercises jurisdiction. The General Court hears cases under arts 263 and 265 TFEU where such cases are brought by natural or legal persons, brought by a Member State against the Commission or brought by a Member State against the Council in relation to state aid, dumping or its exercise of implementing powers.

(3)   Preliminary rulings on the interpretation and validity of European law at the request of a national court or tribunal (art.267 TFEU and art.19(3)(b) TEU). The General Court may assume part of this juridical function in the future.

(4)   Appeals from the General Court on points of law, including, exceptionally, decisions on appeals from the Civil Service Tribunal. Generally, such appeals must take place within two months of the original ruling.

In order to enforce a judgment, the Commission may bring a further infringement action against a Member State under art.260 TFEU. Since 1993, the Court has also been given the power to impose a financial penalty on a Member State if that state still refuses to comply with the Court's judgment or its Treaty obligations (art.260(2) TFEU).

The Court also has jurisdiction to rule on:

- Disputes concerning the European Investment Bank (art.271 TFEU);
- Disputes submitted under special agreements (art.273 TFEU); and
- Compatibility with the Treaties of international agreements entered into by the Union (art.218(11) TFEU; *Opinions* 1/94, 2/94, 1/08, 1/09 and 1/12).

The Court of Justice acts both as a court of first instance and as an appeal court from the General Court.

Its procedure generally falls into four stages (though the second stage is often omitted):

- written proceedings;
- investigation or preparatory inquiry;
- oral proceedings; and
- judgment (the formal ruling of which is published in the Official Journal) and the full judgment together with the Advocate-General's opinion (where applicable), is published in the European Court Reports ("E.C.R.") in all Union languages.

The General Court

To ease the workload of the Court of Justice, the Single European Act provided for the creation of a new Court of First Instance. It began sitting in 1989, with limited jurisdiction—staff cases, competition and anti-dumping cases and some matters relating to the ECSC and Euratom. Since 1993 it has heard all cases brought by natural or legal persons including actions for judicial review and actions for damages against Union institutions or the Member States. The Treaty of Nice introduced a number of changes designed to streamline the workings of the Court. In particular, the Nice Treaty allowed for the development of judicial panels, such as the Civil Service Tribunal (now contained in art.257 TFEU) and offered the possibility of certain aspects of the Preliminary Ruling jurisdiction of the Court of Justice being transferred to it. The Lisbon Treaty continues this reformist trend and also renamed the Court of First Instance as the General Court.

- If there is a serious risk of the unity or consistency of Union law being affected, the General Court's first Advocate-General may propose, within one month of the General Court's decision, that the Court of Justice reviews the decision of the General Court.
- The Court can establish its own Rules of Procedure (art.256(2) and (3) TFEU, and art.62 of Protocol 3 on the Statute of the Court).

The General Court consists of one judge from each Member State appointed under the same criteria as the Judges of the Court of Justice. It may sit with one judge, in chambers of three or five judges, in a Grand Chamber of 13 judges or in plenary session. It has no permanent Advocates-General, with the task of Advocate-General being carried out by one of 28 judges of the General Court. However, the Lisbon Treaty does allow for the General Court to be assisted by Advocates-General in the future (art.254 TFEU).

Jurisdiction of the General Court
To relieve the workload of the Court of Justice, the General Court exercises a wide ranging jurisdiction, as follows:

- contractual and non-contractual liability of the Union (art.340 TFEU; FIAMM [2005]) and compensation for damage in that event (art.268 TFEU; *Abdulrahim v Council and Commission* [2012]);
- actions relating to European Trade Marks;
- appeals against decisions of the Civil Service Tribunal, the Community Plant Variety Office or the European Chemicals Agency;
- direct actions under arts 263 and 265 TFEU, where they are instituted by natural and legal persons, brought by a Member State against the Commission or brought by a Member State against the Council in relation to state aid, dumping or its exercise of implementing powers; and
- arbitration clauses contained in a contract concluded by or on behalf of the Union (art.272 TFEU).

The Civil Service Tribunal
Following the power introduced under the Treaty of Nice to create judicial panels, the Civil Service Tribunal was created in 2004 and commenced work in 2005. The Tribunal consists of seven judges and hears disputes between the EU institutions, bodies and agencies and their respective employees (art.270 TFEU).

COURT OF AUDITORS

The Court of Auditors was set up in 1975 to control and supervise the implementation of the budget. It became a full institution and semi-privileged applicant in 1993 under the Treaty on European Union. Its main function is to scrutinise the Commission's management of the Union budget, examine its legality, regularity of revenue and expenditure and ensure its sound financial management. As an independent audit body (rather than a "court") it is also viewed by Parliament as an essential tool in establishing greater financial control and good management of the Union. On the basis of the Court of Auditors' reports, it is the European Parliament which gives the Commission final discharge for the adoption of the annual budget. It is composed of one full-time member chosen by the Council (after consulting the European Parliament) from each Member State among persons who have had relevant auditing experience and whose independence is beyond doubt.

Its powers and functions are set out in arts 285–287 TFEU.

THE EUROPEAN COUNCIL

The European Council is not to be confused with the Council of the European Union (above) or with the Council of Europe, an international organisation concerned mainly with human rights and based in Strasbourg.

Since 1974, the informal meetings of Heads of State and Government (previously known as "summit meetings") were formalised into biannual meetings hosted by the Member State holding the Presidency of the Union. The President of the Commission also attended these gatherings. Although the European Council possessed no formal powers and thus played no part in the legislative machinery, its meetings have provided momentum for European integration by the injection of political will at the very highest level, to promote co-ordination and clarification of inter-Union relations and set out policy initiatives. It therefore may set out general guidelines for action to be taken at Union level by the Council and the Commission. Its informal discussions also act as a forum for co-ordination of Member States' foreign policies to maximise their influence on world affairs (see art.15 TEU).

The Treaty of Amsterdam introduced new powers for the European Council allowing it to determine the existence of a "serious and persistent breach by a Member State" of the principles of liberty, democracy, respect for human rights and fundamental freedoms, and the rule of law, "after inviting the government of the Member State in question to submit its observations" (art.7.2 TEU).

The Treaty of Lisbon elevated the status of the European Council to that of an institution of the European Union and created the permanent post of President of the European Council, with a term of office of two and a half years. The first holder of this office is Herman van Rompuy. Further, the

European Council now meets four times a year.

The European Council performs a number of important EU functions:

- It provides the Union with the necessary political impetus.
- It represents the EU externally in relation to the Common Foreign and Security Policy ("CFSP") and identifies the strategic interests and objectives of the Union in relation to international issues, including those of defence.
- It can, with Parliament's consent, determine that a member State has engaged in a serious and persistent breach of the Union's values (art.7(2) TEU).
- It proposes to the Parliament the nominee for the post of Commission President and appoints the entire Commission, after obtaining the consent of the Parliament.
- It appoints the High Representative for Foreign Affairs (art.18 TEU) who is tasked with implementing CFSP decisions adopted by the European Council and the Council.
- It has the power to agree, in the future, upon the creation of a common defence (art.42(2) TEU).
- It defines strategic guidelines for legislative and operational planning in respect of the Area of Freedom, Security and Justice (art.68 TFEU).
- It considers the employment situation of the Union on an annual basis and may adopt conclusions on this matter (art.148 TFEU).
- It regularly assesses the threats facing the Union, in particular, those of terrorism and natural and man-made disasters (art.222(4) TFEU).

Accompanied by ever-increasing media attention, the European Council now provides a significant focus of authority and leadership for Europe.

THE EUROPEAN CENTRAL BANK

The European Central Bank became a fully-fledged institution of the EU by virtue of the Treaty of Lisbon. It operates as the central bank for the Euro currency zone, the Eurozone, and is tasked with maintaining the Euro's (€) purchasing power in the Eurozone and thereby promoting price stability. The ECB is therefore solely competent to authorise the issuance of Euro banknotes, with both the ECB and the national central banks operating within the Eurozone authorised to issue Euro banknotes. The issuance of Eurocoins is still a national competence. At present there are seven denominations of Euro banknotes ranging from €5 to €500 and eight demoninations of Euro coins, ranging from one cent to €2 (*Decision of the ECB* [2013] (2013/211/EU). The ECB operates through a Governing Council, which comprises a six-member Executive Board and the 17 governors of the National Central Banks of the member states of the Eurozone. The ECB and the National Central Banks of the Eurozone member states work together as the "Eurosystem" (art.282 TFEU). Alongside the Eurosystem, the European System of Central Banks is the umbrella term for cooperation between the national central banks of the member states that are not in the Eurozone and the participants of the Eurosystem. The national central banks of the member states that have not adopted the Euro are involved in the ESCB through the General Council of the ECB. This body is made up of the President and Vice-President of the ECB and the governors of all 28 national central banks of the member states. The General Council is a temporary body, designed to be dissolved when all member states of the EU have adopted the Euro as their currency.

The on-going financial crisis in the Eurozone has necessitated further regulatory reform and innovation. As such, the EU's financial regulatory system is now augmented by a range of new supervisory bodies, namely: the European Systemic Risk Board; the European Banking Authority; the European Insurance and Occupational Pensions Authority; the European Securities and Markets Authority; and the Joint Committee of the European Supervisory Authorities.

6. EUROPEAN LAW AND NATIONAL LAW

DIRECT EFFECT

The three European Communities were set up through international treaties. International treaties are agreements between states affecting relations between them and do not generally create rights for citizens. However, the European Union legal order differs in that it does create rights within Member States for the nationals of those states, as individuals. Certain provisions of Union law create enforceable private rights for citizens which may be exercised through national courts as if they were part of the law of the land. This individual right is known as "direct effect" and means that individuals can pursue their Union rights through their own local courts. Direct effect was not set out in the founding Treaties, but was developed through the case law of the Court of Justice.

Direct Effect of Treaty Articles
The leading case is still that of *Van Gend en Loos NV v Nederlandse Administratie der Belastingen* [1963]. Van Gend en Loos, a Dutch transport company, imported chemicals from Germany on which it was charged customs duty of 8 per cent of the value of the goods. The company challenged this on the grounds that when the EEC Treaty came into effect in the Netherlands, the duty was only 3 percent and art.12 of the original EEC Treaty required Member States to refrain from introducing any new customs duties on imports and exports of goods—a negative obligation. The Dutch Customs Authorities argued that the Treaty did not allow an individual the right to bring an action on the grounds of infringement of the Treaty. The Court of Justice disagreed and stated that it was necessary to examine the spirit, general scheme and wording of the provision in question. It stated that the EEC Treaty was more than an international agreement which created obligations between states only. It had established a common market and institutions which had been given powers to legislate not only for its Member States but also for individuals. It continued:

> "The [sic] Union constitutes a new legal order of international law for the benefit of which the states have limited their sovereign rights, albeit within limited fields and the subjects of which comprise not only Member States but also their nationals. Independently of the legislation of the Member States, Union law therefore not only imposes obligations on individuals but is also intended to confer on them rights which become part of their legal heritage."

The Court then set out the criteria for direct effect to be applicable. For an individual to rely on a provision of European law within a national court, the provision in question:

- must be sufficiently clear and unambiguous in its terms;
- must be unconditional, that is, not subject to any qualifications; and
- must take effect without any further implementing or discretionary measures either by Member States or by Union institutions.

Van Gend en Loos was soon followed by a number of other similar cases challenging Member States' fulfilment of their Treaty obligations, both negative (refraining from acting in a certain way) and positive (requiring to carry out an action (*Lütticke* [1971])). In such cases, individuals and the state are in a vertical relationship—the state at the apex and the individual beneath, allowing an individual the right to sue a Member State within his own national court when he considers that it has not complied with its EU obligations.

Member State

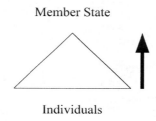

Individuals

Horizontal as well as Vertical Direct Effect?

"Horizontal direct effect", on the other hand, is a relationship between equals—one individual or company—whereby each can sue one another within a national court to assert rights under European law.

Member State

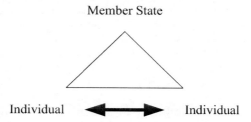

Individual   Individual

In the case of *Defrenne v SABENA* [1976] Ms Defrenne, an air hostess working for the Belgian airline, challenged her employer's policy of compulsorily retiring its female cabin crew, but not its male crew, at the age of 40. Ms Defrenne alleged that this was contrary to art.119 (now art.157 TFEU) covering equal pay. Based on the *Van Gend en Loos* criteria, the Court of Justice stated the provisions of art.119 produced horizontal direct effect and conferred on Ms Defrenne a right to pursue her Union rights under the Treaty against her employer.

Thus if a Treaty Article satisfies the three criteria set out in the *Van Gend en Loos* case it will produce direct effect—vertical and horizontal—and may be relied upon by individuals. Through the continuing jurisprudence of the Court, Treaty Articles concerning the free movement of goods, persons, equal pay and competition now possess the character of direct effect and allow individuals to pursue their Union rights through their own national courts.

Direct Effect of Regulations

Regulations generally apply automatically within Member States without any need for domestic implementing measures. A regulation becomes law when it is published in the Official Journal. Article 288 TFEU states that, "a regulation ... shall be ... directly applicable in all Member States". Direct applicability, however, does *not* necessarily mean that regulations are directly effective, that is they grant individuals rights which can be enforced and protected through the national courts. They still have to satisfy the Van Gend en Loos criteria before this is so (*Marimex* [1972]; *Munoz* [2002]).

All that direct applicability means is that there is no need for further legislation to be enacted by Member States incorporating the EU provision into national law. Indeed, for a Member State to do so, will engage the principle of State Liability, since the Member State, by its actions, is disguising the true source of the legal obligation set out in the Regulation (*Commission v Italy (The Slaughtered Cow)* [1973]). However, there may be instances where national administrative measures will be necessary in order to give further effect to the Regulation (*Commission v UK (Tachographs)* [1973]; *Horvath* [2009]; and *Rakvere Piim* [2011]).

Direct Effect of Decisions

Article 288 TFEU sets out a decision as being, "binding in its entirety upon those to whom it is addressed". In practice a decision can be addressed to one or more Member States or one or more individuals. If a decision which is addressed to a Member State fulfils the *Van Gend en Loos* criteria it can also possess direct effect and give rights to individuals (*Grad* [1970]).

Direct Effect of Directives

It must be stressed at this juncture that directives are never directly applicable and were never designed to be. Article 288 TFEU states that, "a directive shall be binding as to the result to be achieved" but that the choice of "form and methods" is left to the Member State (*Commission v Estonia* [2012]). Directives thus always require some enacting measure to be carried out and may entail a wide measure of discretion on the part of the Member State. A logical consequence flowing from the existence of this autonomy for the Member States in choosing how to implement EU law obligations is that devolved administrations within a Member State must be free to implement these EU law obligations in a different way from that of other regions within the same Member State (*Horvath* [2009]; and *Dept. of the Environment for Northern Ireland v Seaport* [2011]). Moreover, art.291(1)

TFEU explicitly provides that "Member States shall adopt all measures of national law necessary to implement legally binding Union acts". Nevertheless, under certain conditions directives may be directly effective, on the basis that failure to implement a directive is a failure to grant citizens of a Member State their rights under the EU Treaties. Such inaction is discriminatory, a violation of both the "good faith" clause of art.4(3) TEU and art.291(1) TFEU and offends against the principle of personal bar/estoppel. In the case of *Grad*, as the time limit for implementation had expired, the provisions of the directive in question requiring Member States to amend their VAT systems could produce direct effect.

In the case of *Van Duyn v Home Office* [1974], the Court examined the wording, nature and general scheme of Directive 64/221 on which Ms Van Duyn relied and stated that a clear and precise obligation had been set out which was not subject to the adoption of subsequent acts on the part either of the Union or of Member States. Finally, the directive imposed a specific limitation on the discretion of the Member State in the field of public security. Ms Van Duyn's challenge to the Member State (the United Kingdom) was allowed by the Court because the effectiveness (*effet utile*) of the directive would be weakened if individuals were unable to enforce rights conferred on them through the courts. However, it should be noted that direct effect of directives may be relied upon only:

- after the expiry of the time allowed for its implementation into national law by the Member State (*Ratti* [1978]);
- if the Directive satisfies the three criteria of *Van Gend en Loos*; and
- where the Member State has either not implemented the directive or has incorrectly or incompletely transposed the terms of the directive into national law (*Becker* [1982]; *Emmot* [1990]).

Horizontal as well as Vertical Direct Effect for Directives?

In *Marshall v Southampton Area Health Authority* [1986] the Court had to ascertain whether Directive 79/7 could be relied upon not only against the state but also against another individual or company, as in the *Defrenne* case—in other words, whether directives could be said to have horizontal as well as vertical direct effect. Miss Marshall had sued her employer whose policy compelled women to retire at 60, five years earlier than male retirement age. The Court of Justice was asked to rule on whether the directive had direct effect and if so, whether this could be horizontal as well as vertical. The Court pointed out that directives are only binding on the Member State to whom they addressed and that therefore "a Directive may not of itself, impose obligations on an individual" and "may not be relied upon as such against such a person", but found that Member States had responsibilities towards individuals not simply as public authorities but as employers. It found that the Area Health Authority was an "organ of the state" and that this phrase would cover all organs of the administration including Miss Marshall's employer, as part of the National Health Service. In this case, Miss Marshall was able to rely on the directive as having vertical direct effect.

In a series of subsequent cases, the Court continued to interpret the meaning of "organ of the state" as widely as possible to minimise the inequalities arising when individuals attempted to assert their Union rights against their employers and to prevent a Member State from relying as a defence on its own failure. Difficulties revolved round the question of whether the employer was a public authority (in which case an employee would be allowed to pursue a case based on the vertical direct effect of a directive) rather than a private business (where the employee would not be able to pursue their Union rights at all). See also:

- *Foster v British Gas Plc* [1990]. This concerned a case brought in pursuance of rights guaranteed by the Equal Treatment Directive 76/207. The Court held that British Gas—a nationalised industry at that time rather than a private company—was an organ of the state as it was offering a public service under the control of a public authority, and was therefore open to challenge through vertical direct effect.
- *Johnston v Chief Constable of the Royal Ulster Constabulary* [1986]. It was held that a directive could be relied upon against a chief constable as he was responsible to the public for the maintenance of order and safety and was not acting as a private individual.

It was by now quite clear that an individual could pursue rights conferred by an unimplemented directive against a Member State through the doctrine of vertical direct effect. But inequalities of treatment depending on the status of the employer/alleged infringer remained. This was aggravated by Member States sometimes incorporating directives into national law using precisely the same wording as the original, thus giving them the appearance of regulations.

In *Faccini Dori v Recreb Srl* [1994] when the Court was asked once again to rule on horizontal direct effect, it resolved the uncertainty once and for all. It emphasised that extending the doctrine of direct effect of directives to individuals would be "to recognise a power in the Union to enact obligations with immediate effect"; a power which previously only related to regulations. To attribute horizontal direct effect to directives would therefore establish that they had the same legal effect as regulations. However, a Directive may produce effects analogous to horizontal direct effect in a very narrow and specific range of circumstances. This "incidental" horizontal direct effect, as it is called, may apply where there is a triangular relationship between the applicant, the state and other specified individuals who will be affected by the court decision (*CIA Security* [1996]; *Unilever* [2000]). However, the successful case law in this area appears to be limited to cases under Directive 83/189 and its replacement, Directive 98/34. Both these Directives require that Member States notify the Commission of national law technical standards and regulations that apply to goods. Where national law has not been notified in breach of the directive, that national law cannot be relied upon, although minor technical changes to national law provisions that actually improve the free movement of goods do not need to be notified to the Commission (*Sandström* [2010]).

This case law is highly controversial in that the practical effect is that the legal position of individuals is directly affected by the provisions of the directive. The case law, therefore, must be treated with caution and should be viewed as a very narrow exception to the general rule that directives can never produce horizontal direct effect.

Although directives do not have horizontal direct effect, this does not mean that individuals are without legal redress. Rather, individuals may enforce their rights under a directive through the concept of indirect effect or through the *Francovich* principles of state liability (see under Member State Liability).

Indirect Effect
Despite the Court's insistence that provisions of Union law must have *effet utile*, the main limitations on the direct effect of directives are that legally binding European legislation:

- must fulfil the *Van Gend en Loos* criteria—be sufficiently precise, unconditional and not involve discretion in the method of implementation;
- cannot have direct effect until the time limit for implementation has expired;
- cannot have direct effect unless a Member State has failed to implement or has incorrectly implemented the provisions of the directive into national law; and
- does not have horizontal direct effect.

The Court therefore created an obligation on national courts to interpret national law in such a way as to achieve the aim of the directive. This approach—known as indirect effect—is based on art.4(3) TEU which requires Member States to "take any appropriate measure, general or particular, to ensure fulfilment of the obligations arising out of the Treaties or resulting from the acts of the institutions of the Union".

In the case of *Von Colson und Kamman v Land Nordrhein-Westfalen* [1984] challenge was made under the Equal Treatment Directive 76/207. The Court of Justice found that the directive was not sufficiently precise and unconditional to possess direct effect but invoked (old) art.5 which placed Member States under an obligation to fulfil their Treaty obligations, stating that national implementing legislation had to be sufficient "such as to guarantee real and effective judicial protection" and that, "it was for the national court to interpret and apply the legislation adopted ... in conformity with the requirements of Union law, insofar as it is given discretion to do so under national law".

This approach was extended in *Marleasing SA v La Commercial Internacional de Alimentacion SA* [1990], a case brought by one company against another. As well as reiterating the prohibition against horizontal direct effect, the Court repeated the obligation on national courts to interpret national legislation whether adopted before or after the directive as far as possible in the light of the wording and purpose of the directive (*Uniplex (UK)* [2010].

The interpretative obligation has proved problematic for national courts in the situation where they are obliged to interpret national legislation that predates a directive (*Litster v Forth Dry Dock Engineering* [1990]). Nevertheless, the Court of Justice has consistently held that the interpretative obligation applies regardless of whether the disputed national law was enacted before or after the European law and whether it was enacted for the purpose of complying with EU law or not. Clearly, there are limits to the appropriateness and usefulness of this interpretative obligation, especially in the situation where national law expressly contradicts the Directive (*Wagner Miret* [1993]).

The Court of Justice has also made it clear that indirect effect cannot be used in criminal proceedings (*Kolpinghuis Nijmegen* [1987]; *Arcaro* [1996]).

Additionally, the Court has confirmed that during the period in which Member States have discretion to implement national law to give effect to the directive, they must refrain from taking action which undermines the aims and objectives of the directive and/or the treaties (*Mangold* [2006]).

Direct Effect of Recommendations and Opinions
Since Recommendations and Opinions do not produce binding legal effects, they cannot produce direct effects (*Grimaldi* [1989]).

MEMBER STATE LIABILITY

After a series of cases in which horizontal direct effect was denied, the Court then turned in a different direction to protect individuals' Union rights. Individuals who had suffered as a result of a Member State's failure to fulfil its Union obligations had at that stage little redress in law, other than to rely on a national court making a preliminary reference to the European Court of Justice on the interpretation of the Treaty.

In 1991, with the landmark case of *Francovich*, it began to build a system of Member State liability as a default position to provide effective rights for individuals. The principle of Member State liability places an obligation upon a defaulting Member State to recompense individuals in damages for its own failure. Although in *Francovich*, Directive 80/987 (on the protection of workers in the event of the insolvency of their employer) was held not to be directly effective, the Court held that the protection of Union rights would be weakened if individuals were unable to obtain any effective remedy when their rights were infringed by a breach of Union law for which a Member State could be held responsible. It laid down three conditions to be fulfilled before a Member State might be found to be liable in damages even if the measure was not directly effective:

- the directive must confer rights for the benefits of individuals;
- the content of the rights must be identifiable from the directive; and
- there must be a causal link between the damage suffered and the breach.

The Court did not decide how the extent of liability was to be determined. This was to be a matter for the national courts to determine—though national procedures had "to ensure the full protection of rights which individuals might derive from Union law".

The implications of the *Francovich* judgment were that Member States faced the possibility of paying compensation to individuals if they failed to implement a directive in time. But some areas of doubt remained—whether any other type of breach of Union law by Member States other than a failure to implement a directive would lead to Member States incurring liability in damages; and secondly, whether "fault" was necessary in order to incur liability.

Where the Court has found a Member State to have a wide discretion, that is to say the competent national authorities have substantive choices in how they can act under Union law, it has applied the *Factortame (No.3)* conditions. These were set out in joined cases *Brasserie du Pêcheur v Germany* and *R v Secretary of State for Transport, Ex p. Factortame* [1996] in which the Court considered claims for compensation as a result of conflicting national and Union law. These conditions were that:

- the rule of law infringed must be intended to confer rights on individuals;
- the breach must be sufficiently serious; and
- there must be a direct causal link between the breach of the obligation resting on the state and the damage sustained by the injured parties.

The requirements for establishing state liability are clearly similar to those arising from *Francovich* with the added requirement of establishing a "sufficiently serious" breach. The Court clarified what it meant by this and provided guidelines for national courts to evaluate whether or not a breach was sufficiently serious as follows:

- How clear and precise was the rule which was breached?
- Did national authorities have any discretion in its implementation?
- Was the breach intentional?
- Was the error of law excusable?
- Had a Union institution contributed to the breach?

The decisive test on whether or not a breach was sufficiently serious would be whether or not the Member State had manifestly and gravely disregarded the limits of its discretion.

In *R v Ministry of Agriculture, Fisheries and Food, Ex p. Hedley Lomas (Ireland) Ltd* [1994] the Court applied the *Factortame (No.3)* conditions. The Ministry of Agriculture, Fisheries and Food had refused licences for the exporting of livestock to Spain because it believed that Spain was acting contrary to Directive 74/557. The United Kingdom was held to have breached Union law by imposing an export ban contrary to art.34 TFEU. It had clearly acted in the face of Union law and accordingly was liable in damages to Hedley Lomas.

In *R v HM Treasury, Ex p. British Telecommunications Plc* [1996] the issue was the incorrect implementation of a directive by the United Kingdom where it clearly did not have wide discretion in its Union obligation to implement a directive correctly. In this case though, the directive at issue was imprecisely worded and the UK had acted in good faith. The breach was held not to be sufficiently serious enough to incur liability for damages.

However, in *Dillenkofer v Federal Republic of Germany* [1996] Germany had failed to implement Directive 90/314 in time. The type of breach was therefore similar to that in *Francovich*. The Court went on to apply the *Factortame (No.3)* conditions rather than the original *Francovich* conditions, thus indicating that it regarded the conditions relating to state liability to be fixed no matter what the nature of the breach was. In this case, it stated that the very nature of Germany's breach of Union law—a complete disregard of its obligations—was sufficiently serious.

To provide an effective mechanism for the enforcement of individuals' rights, ensure consistent application of Union law throughout the Member States and to encourage Member States to be vigilant in their application of Union law, the Court of Justice has now established that the requirements for state liability are that:

(1) Based on a Member State's obligations under art.4(3) TEU, it must "take any appropriate measures ... to ensure fulfilment of the obligations arising out of the Treaties ... (and) facilitate the achievement of the Union's tasks and refrain from any measure which could jeopardise the attainment of the Union's objectives".

(2) A breach of Union law is sufficiently serious where, in the exercise of its legislative powers, a Member State has manifestly and gravely disregarded the limits on the exercise of its powers. If, at the time when it committed the infringement, the Member State in question did not have legislative choices and had only considerably reduced, or even no discretion, the mere infringement of Union law may be sufficient to establish the existence of a sufficiently serious breach (*Factortame (No.4)* [1996]).

(3) The nature of a sufficiently serious breach of a Member State's obligations does not necessarily require to be non-implementation

of a directive. Such a breach could include instances of actions by a Member State:

- after a judgment by the Court finding it in breach of Union law;
- where it had persisted in its actions despite that judgment;
- where it had taken no action to implement a directive; and
- where it had acted (or omitted to act) in the face of established Union law.

(4) Fault—whether negligent or intentional—is not one of the conditions which it is necessary to satisfy in order for state liability to be established, especially since the concept of "fault" may differ throughout the various legal systems of the Member States.

(5) It is for the national courts to determine whether a breach of Union law is sufficiently serious to incur the non-contractual liability of a Member State vis-à-vis individuals.

Thus, state liability has developed to become a significant principle of EU law that is of general application, when there is any question raised concerning Member State failure to fulfil EU obligations. The principle binds all divisions of a Member State, that is the executive, the legislature and the judiciary (*Köbler* [2003]; *Traghetti* [2006]) and also extends to devolved administrative organs and public law bodies (*Haim* [2000]). The Court has also had occasion to condemn national procedural rules which make it more difficult for individuals to sue the State for damages in cases involving the question of Member State Liability. National procedural rules must be effective and provide for equivalent treatment of cases either based on alleged violations of national law or of EU law (*Transportes Urbanos* [2010]).

SUPREMACY

Creating an effective legal system to apply directly within the Member States in a uniform and consistent manner would be of little value if Member States themselves could enact conflicting measures which would override Union law or choose which Union rules they would—or would not—apply. Nor were the founding Treaties of any assistance, as they contained no express provision on how to deal with the possibility of a conflict between a rule of Union law and national provisions. The basis of the Court's deduction of the supremacy of Union law therefore was to rely on what is now art.4(3) TEU, which sets out the obligations of the Member States to ensure the effectiveness of the Treaties and associated secondary legislation. The proposed European Constitution would have inserted an article on supremacy into the Constitution, but the Treaty of Lisbon merely provided for a declaration confirming the supremacy of EU law to be attached to the Treaties. Thus, supremacy remains a judicial construct. However, certain provisions of the Treaty indirectly relate to and bolster the concept of supremacy. For example, art.344 TFEU provides that Member States must submit disputes between them to the Court of Justice of the European Union (*Commission v Ireland* [2006]).

In the case of *Costa v ENEL* [1964] Mr Costa challenged a small electricity bill from the Italian State electricity authority, arguing that the Italian legislation nationalising the electricity industry infringed both the Italian Constitution and the provisions of the EEC Treaty. In a much quoted statement, the Court held that:

> "By creating a [*sic*] Union of unlimited duration, having its own institutions, its own personality, its own legal capacity and capacity of representation on the international plane and more particularly, real powers stemming from a limitation of sovereignty or a transfer of powers from the States of the [*sic*] Union, the Member States have limited their sovereign rights, albeit within limited fields, and have thus created a body of law which binds both their nationals and themselves. The integration into the laws of each Member States of provisions which derive from the [sic.] Union , and more generally the terms and the spirit of the Treaty *make it impossible for the States,* as a corollary, *to accord precedence to a unilateral and subsequent measure over a legal system accepted by them.*" [emphasis added]

The supremacy of Union law was given further weight in *Internationale Handelsgesellschaft* [1970] and in *Simmenthal* [1977] in which the Court went further and stated that:

> "Any National Court must ... apply [*sic*] Union law in its entirety ... and must accordingly set aside any provision of national law which may conflict with it, whether prior or subsequent to the [*sic*] Union rule."

In the United Kingdom, the European Communities Act 1972 (as amended, most recently in 2013) provides for the supremacy of Union law by accepting the legal effect of Union provisions in the United Kingdom, as a matter of national law. (See also s.18 European Union Act 2011.) The 1972 Act is generally viewed as having a constitutional status, precluding application of the doctrine of implied repeal (*Thoburn* [2002]). Supremacy similarly extends to judgments of the Court of Justice concerning interpretation on the meaning and effect, or validity of any Union measure. In relation to Acts of the UK Parliament, this means that directly applicable Union measures prevail even over future Acts of Parliament, if the latter are inconsistent with Union law. It also means that by ratifying the European Treaties, the United Kingdom, like any other Member State, must refrain from enacting legislation inconsistent with Union law. In 1991, in *Factortame (No.2)* the Court of Justice replied to a question put by the UK House of Lords:

"[*sic*] Union law must be interpreted as meaning that a national court which, in a case before it concerning [*sic*] Union law, considers that the sole obstacle which precludes it from granting interim relief is a rule of national law, must set aside that rule."

Nevertheless, accepting supremacy of Union law—whether a Treaty article, secondary legislation or agreement with a third state (*Soysal and Savatli* [2009])—has raised difficulties in some Member States over the years, particularly with respect to previously enacted national law or the provisions of a Member State's own constitution (European Union Amendment Act 2008 and European Union Act 2011).

The role of the Court of Justice was pivotal in settling the issues which arose. Interpreting Union law was entrusted by the treaties solely to the Court and through its case law the concept of primacy of Union law now means that:

- states have agreed through their membership of the European Union to the limitation of their sovereign rights, *Costa v ENEL* [1964];
- European Union law may not be invalidated by any provisions of national constitutions, *Internationale Handelsgesellschaft* [1970];
- previously enacted but conflicting national law must be repealed, *Commission v France (re French Merchant Seamen)* [1974];
- European Union law must be applied immediately without waiting for inconsistent national law to be repealed, *Simmenthal* [1977];
- Member States may generally not plead force majeure, *Commission v Italy (Second Art Treasures case)* [1971] and (*Waste Management*) [2010];
- supremacy applies regardless of whether the inconsistent national law is civil or criminal in nature, *Procureur du Roi v Dassonville* [1974];
- national courts should interpret national legislation so as to comply with the Member State's Union obligations whether the national law is passed before or after the relevant provision of Union law, *Marleasing* [1990]; and
- this obligation must not be applied retrospectively to penalise individuals, *Kolpinghuis Nijmegen* [1987].

SUBSIDIARITY

In an attempt to demonstrate that the relationship between Union law and national law was not one which irrevocably transferred the centre of power from national governments to Union institutions, in 1993 the Treaty on European Union formally introduced the principle of subsidiarity into EU law. Following Lisbon, art.5(3) TEU now sets out that:

"Under the principle of subsidiarity, in areas which do not fall within its exclusive competence, the Union shall act only if and insofar as the objectives of the proposed action cannot be sufficiently achieved by Member States, either at central level or at regional and local level, but can rather, by reason of the scale or effects of the proposed action, be better achieved at Union level."

In essence, this means that the choice of legislative or other action is required to be taken in favour of Member States in cases where:

- legislative or other action required to be taken can be taken by either the Member States or the Union, that is the power is shared;
- the Treaties did not specify that the Union possessed the power to act;
- the powers could be exercised by a Member State more effectively and in proportion to the objective pursued; and
- the need for action at Union level could not be demonstrated.

Conversely, the Union should take action where:

- the issue under consideration has transnational aspects which cannot be satisfactorily regulated by action by Member States;
- actions by Member States alone or lack of Union action would conflict with the requirements of the Treaties (such as the need to correct distortion of competition or avoid disguised restrictions on trade or strengthen economic and social cohesion) or would otherwise significantly damage Member States' interests; and
- action at Union level would produce clear benefits by reason of its scale or effects compared with action at the level of the Member States.

In such a case, the form of Union action should be as simple as possible and should leave as much scope for national decision making as possible, consistent with securing the aim of the measure and the need for effective enforcement. Additionally, the Union should legislate only to the extent necessary. In the face of some confusion over aspects of the application of this principle, a Protocol on the Application of the Principles of Subsidiarity and Proportionality was attached to the Treaty of Amsterdam. This protocol has been superseded by the new Protocol on Subsidiarity and Proportionality and the Protocol on Information for the National Parliaments attached to the Treaty of Lisbon. These new Protocols outline a far larger role for national parliaments in ensuring that the terms of subsidiarity are satisfied. The Subsidiarity Protocol requires the Commission to consult widely before submitting legislative proposals and must justify the relevance of its proposals with regard to subsidiarity and detail this in its explanatory memorandum. These legislative proposals, or indeed legislative proposals submitted by the other EU institutions or the

Member States, must then be sent to the national parliaments for scrutiny, with the national parliaments having eight weeks to debate whether subsidiarity is being complied with (arts 3 and 4 of Protocol 1 on Information for the National Parliaments). If a third of national parliaments object to the proposal, the Commission or the organisation which submitted the draft legislation must review the proposal (colloquially known as the "yellow" card) and must decide whether to maintain, amend or withdraw the proposal. For proposals that progress to the ordinary legislative procedure stage, the Commission is obliged to review the proposal where more than half of the national parliaments object and thereafter, the Commission must decide whether to maintain, amend or withdraw the proposal (the "orange" card) (art.7(2) and (3) of Protocol 2 on Subsidiarity and Proportionality).

Compliance with art.4.3 TEU of the Commission's proposals must be specifically addressed by the Council and the European Parliament during the passage of legislation. In the preamble to the measure in question, reasons demonstrating its compliance with the principles of subsidiarity and proportionality must be set out. More generally, the Commission must submit an annual report on the application of subsidiarity to the European Council, the Council and to the European and national parliaments (art.9 of Protocol 2).

Even where the legislative proposal successfully overcomes these subsidiarity hurdles, the resultant legislation may subsequently be subject to a subsidiarity challenge under art.263 TFEU (see Ch.7 below and art.8 of Protocol 2).

7. JUDICIAL REVIEW

To protect the rights of individuals and Member States, the Treaties provide for an extensive system of judicial review to ensure that Union institutions fulfil their obligations under the Treaties in a proper manner. Based on French administrative law, judicial review also safeguards the rights of the institutions in their dealings with one another. The Treaty confers specific powers and duties on each of the institutions which they must exercise according to the Treaty:

- Under art.263 TFEU, the Court of Justice may consider an action for annulment of an act of the institutions.
- Article 265 TFEU provides the means by which an institution's failure to act may be investigated.

Article 277 TFEU provides a means of indirect review where the "plea of illegality" is invoked. By far the most important of these three is the action for annulment under art.263 TFEU.

ACTION FOR ANNULMENT UNDER ARTICLE 263 TFEU

Article 263

"The Court of Justice of the European Union shall review the legality of legislative acts, of acts of the Council, of the Commission and of the European Central Bank, other than recommendations and opinions, and of acts of the European Parliament and of the European Council intended to produce legal effects vis-à-vis third parties.

It shall also review the legality of acts of bodies, offices or agencies of the Union intended to produce legal effects *vis-à-vis* third parties. It shall for this purpose have jurisdiction in actions brought by a Member State, the European Parliament, the Council or the Commission on grounds of lack of competence, infringement of an essential procedural requirement, infringement of the Treaties or of any rule of law relating to their application, or misuse of powers.

The Court shall have jurisdiction under the same conditions in actions brought by the Court of Auditors, by the European Central Bank and by the Committee of the Regions for the purpose of protecting their prerogatives.

Any natural or legal person may, under the conditions laid down in the first and second paragraphs, institute proceedings against an act addressed to that person or which is of direct and individual concern to them, and against a regulatory act which is of direct concern to them and does not entail implementing measures.

Acts setting up bodies, offices and agencies of the Union may lay down specific conditions and arrangements concerning actions brought by natural or legal persons against acts of these bodies, offices or agencies intended to produce legal effects in relation to them.

The proceedings provided for in this Article shall be instituted within two months of the publication of the measure, or of its notification to the plaintiff, or, in the absence thereof, of the day on which it came to the knowledge of the latter, as the case may be."

In order to be successful, the action for annulment brought under art.263 TFEU must clear two hurdles. The first is the admissibility requirement. This means that the applicant must first satisfy the Court that he or she (or it, in the case of a business) is allowed to bring the action in the first place and that it is laid down within the time limits. This is known as locus standi. Second, the applicant must then convince the Court that the challenge is on one of the grounds for review which is allowed under art.263 TFEU.

Actions under art.263 TFEU are instituted in the Court of Justice, with the exception of actions brought by natural or legal persons, brought by a Member State against the Commission or brought by a Member State against the Council in relation to state aid, dumping or its exercise of implementing powers (*Spain and Italy v Council* [2013]). These latter actions must be raised in the General Court.

To found a successful action, five questions must be addressed.

(1) Which Acts may be Challenged?
Anything which is legally binding—regulations, decisions, directives, but not recommendations and opinions (see art.288 TFEU). However, these forms of legislation are not all that may be challenged. Because the Court of Justice is concerned with the substance of a measure rather than the form it takes, it will consider all measures taken by the EU institutions, bodies, offices and agencies which are designed to have legal effect (*Rutgers* [2013]). In *Commission v Council (re ERTA)* [1971] "discussions" of guidelines before the signing of the European Road Traffic Agreement were held to be capable of review by the Court. Further, in *European Parliament v Council* [1994] the Court stated that:

"Annulment must be available in the case of all measures adopted by the institutions, whatever their nature or form, intended to have legal effects. It follows that an action ... is admissible irrespective of whether the act was adopted by the institution pursuant to the Treaty provisions."

However, in *IBM v Commission* [1981] the company challenged a letter and Statement of Objections sent by the Commission in pursuance of competition rules. As this was only the first step of several in an enforcement procedure, the Court held that this could not be challenged. Only a final measure may be challenged (*Co-Frutta v Commission* [2010]).

(2) Who has the Right to Challenge?

A distinction is drawn between institutional and private applicants— between what are referred to as privileged applicants, semi-privileged applicants and non-privileged applicants.

Privileged applicants are the Member States, the Council, the Commission and the European Parliament. They have an automatic right to challenge any legal measure as they are presumed to have an interest in any Union proceedings (*Luxembourg v European Parliament* [1983]).

Semi-privileged applicants are the European Central Bank, the Court of Auditors and the Committee of the Regions. They have a limited right to challenge measures, but only if they can demonstrate a specific interest in the proceedings and are taking action to safeguard their prerogatives (*European Parliament v Council* [1991]).

Private individuals and companies (natural or legal persons)—that is, non-privileged applicants—may challenge a Union act, but only if this act is:

- A decision addressed to that person. This means that there is an obvious and straightforward right of challenge. If the addressee of the contested decision brings an action within the time limit, the claim will be admissible;
- A decision addressed to another person or to a Member State. In this case, the applicant must show that the act in question is of direct and individual concern to them (*Fiskano v Commission* [1994]); and
- A regulatory act which is of direct concern to them and does not entail implementing measures.

A measure is of direct concern to an applicant when a Member State is given no discretion to act under the disputed provision or when there is no implementing measure required to be acted upon by the Member State and the measure directly affects the legal situation of the individual (*Glencore Grain* [1998]; *Regione Siciliana v Commission* [2007]). In *Bock* [1971] despite the fact that the German authorities had already informed the applicant that they would reject his application for an import licence for Chinese mushrooms as soon as the Commission allowed them to do so, it was held that Germany's discretion whether or not to authorise the import licence was not at issue as the Commission had upheld a refusal in response to Bock's application. Bock was held to be directly concerned.

It is of individual concern if it affects the applicant in the same way as if it had been addressed to him personally, either alone or as a member of a closed class. The test is that in *Plaumann* [1963]. Plaumann was a fruit importer. A decision sent by the Commission to Germany refused permission to reduce the duty on clementines imported from outside the Union. Plaumann challenged the Commission's decision. That his business would be affected was not sufficient to constitute "individual concern". The Court said the measure was a response to a general problem and drafted accordingly, without special reference to any individual trader, present or potential. Plaumann was merely an importer and as anyone could set up in business as an importer, Plaumann was not therefore individually concerned, since the potential pool of individuals affected by the measure was open.

Although most applicants seeking to prove individual concern are unsuccessful, in the case of *Töpfer*, an importer of grain and cereals had requested a licence on October 1, 1963 from the German Government so that he could import cereals from France. He was refused permission and the Commission was asked to confirm this decision which it did, retrospectively, on October 4. The Court said that the identity of the applicant had been known to the Commission before October 4 and it was therefore in a position to know that its decision affected the interests of existing importers. This fact distinguished Töpfer since he was a member of a closed group of affected individuals. Töpfer was therefore individually concerned and accordingly his action was admissible.

In Bock's case in 1971, the Court held that the company was individually concerned because the application made to import Chinese mushrooms was made on September 11, refused by Germany on the same date, but upheld by the Commission on September 15. The number and identity of importers concerned was already fixed and ascertainable before the refusal by the Commission on September 15 and it was in a position to know that its decision would affect the interests and situation of those importers alone.

The 1985 case of *Piraiki-Patriki* concerned seven Greek cotton companies which challenged a Commission decision allowing the French Government to impose a quota system on imports of yarn from Greece between November 1981 and January 1982. Some of the applicants had already signed contracts with French companies for deliveries above the quota during that period. The Court held that the decision was of individual concern to those of the applicants who had signed the contracts as they were "members of a limited class of traders identified or identifiable by the Commission and by reason of these contracts, particularly affected by the decision".

However, in the case of *Codorniu* in 1994, the Court of Justice developed its approach to "individual concern" further. The measure in question was in the form of a regulation made by the Council which reserved the term "crémant" for particular types of sparkling wine produced in France and Luxembourg. The applicant was a major producer of sparkling wines in Spain, one of the largest producers of sparkling wine in Europe and had held a Spanish trademark since 1924 for its Gran Crémant wine. The Court held that the measure was a true regulation of general application and, although Codorniu was not one of a fixed and ascertainable group, he was distinguished from other producers as he would be deprived of the trademark right which he had held for the previous 70 years.

The Court reverted to its more restrictive approach as set out in *Plaumann* in the case of *Stichting Greenpeace Council* in 1998 which seemed to indicate that it was still difficult to get past the locus standi hurdle. Greenpeace had challenged a Commission decision to allocate financial aid to Spain to build two power stations in the Canary Islands on environmental grounds. The Court held that "the interests [of the local residents, fishermen and farmers] are by their very nature, common and shared, and the rights relating to these are liable to be held by a potentially large number of individuals so there could never be a closed class of applicants".

These restrictive rules on locus standi for private applicants remained unchanged until the Lisbon Treaty. In practice it has been almost impossible for an individual to satisfy the admissibility test for a challenge under art.263 TFEU, thus the need for reform of this area of law has periodically surfaced over the years. Notwithstanding the specific case of *Codorniu*, the first serious attempt to generally relax the standing rules came in the guise of *Jégo-Quéré et Cie* [2002]. In that case, the Court of First Instance deviated from the prior case law, relaxing the previously restrictive application of "individual concern". However, later that year, the Court of Justice in *Unión de Pequeños Agricultores* [2002] reiterated that the pre-*Jégo-Quéré* case law was still to apply. It emphasised that it was not for the Court to reform the conditions for locus standi and that if Member States wished to liberalise the rules regulating the right of individuals to challenge Union measures, then it would have to be secured by way of Treaty amendment. The requisite Treaty amendment came about under the Lisbon Treaty. However, the relaxation contained in Lisbon is not without its difficulties. First, the test of "direct and individual" concern is retained in respect of decisions, with only challenges directed at regulatory acts benefiting from the relaxed requirement to only prove direct concern.

Regulations, directives and decisions may be legislative or non-legislative in nature, as per arts 290 and 297(2) TFEU. The term "regulatory act" cannot include directives since they entail implementing measures (*Arcelor* [2010]). In any event, directives are, in principle, challengeable by natural and legal persons under art.263 TFEU (*Japan Tobacco* [2002]) and, more generally, Member States are also required to ensure that they provide "remedies sufficient to ensure effective legal protection" in relation to EU law (art.19(1) TEU). Thus, domestic law must also offer the possibility of indirect challenges to the validity of EU law.

In a similar vein, the Court of Justice has held that the term "regulatory act" cannot extend to legislative regulations, that is regulations adopted under the legislative procedures set out in the treaties (*Inuit Tapiriit Kanatami* [2011]). Thus, the liberalisation of the standing rules only applies to EU Regulations that are non-legislative in nature and of general application, for example anti-dumping Regulations in the field of competition law, since to open up challenges to general legislation by anyone "directly concerned" would be to potentially open the floodgates to a plethora of vexatious or frivolous court actions (*Microban* [2011]; *Eurofer* [2012]; and *Rutgers* [2013]). Conversely, even if liberalisation of the standing rules were to be extended to cover all types of "regulatory acts", the floodgates may still prove difficult to open if the criteria for "direct concern" are more tightly applied.

(3) What are the Grounds for Challenge?
Lack of Competence
The Treaties require each of the Union institutions to act within the limits of the powers conferred upon it (*Menidiatis* [2009]). Thus, in the *ERTA* case [1971], it was obvious to the Court that the Council lacked the power to negotiate the European Road Transport Agreement, as old art.300 stated that the Commission negotiated international agreements and the Council concluded them. It follows that every act of a Union institution must clearly indicate on which Treaty provision it is based (*Germany v EP and Council (Tobacco Advertising)* [2000]).

Infringement of an Essential Procedural Requirement
Institutions adopting binding measures must adhere to the correct procedures as laid down either in the Treaties or within secondary legislation implemented in accordance with the Treaties. The leading case, *Roquette Frères* [1980], concerned a requirement for Parliament to be consulted in a legal measure. "Failure to consult" annulled the measure in question.

"Failure to give sufficient reasons" may also be grounds for annulment of a binding measure. This ground of review is normally pleaded when an institution has not given reasons for its adoption of binding legal measures (*Commission v Council Re Titanium Dioxide Waste* [1991]). The measure must therefore specify the principal issues of fact and law in a clear and concise manner so that the reasoning which led the institution to make its choice of legal basis may be clearly understood.

Infringement of the Treaty or of any Rule relating to its Application
This ground of challenge is interpreted broadly because it covers not only the Treaties and their implementing legislation, but also general principles of law such as:

- equality (*R Louwage v Commission* [1974]);
- legal certainty (*Openbaar Ministerie v Bout* [1982]);
- proportionality (*Commission v Germany* [1994]);
- fundamental rights, including those set out in the Charter; and
- legitimate expectation (*Töpfer* [1965]).

Misuse of Powers
This refers to an act of an institution endeavouring to achieve an objective which is not that for which the original powers were conferred upon it

(*Giuffrida v Commission* [1976]; *Wenning* [2009]). The Court will examine:

- the purpose the act was intended to achieve; and
- the purpose of the provision under which the act was adopted, to see if the act followed this purpose.

This ground is the most difficult to prove as evidence is required that the intention of the institution in question was different from that stated in the contested measure (*Crispoltoni* [1994]).

(4) What are the Relevant Time Limits?
The Court enforces the time limits very strictly. An applicant—whether privileged or non-privileged—must bring a claim within two months of the date of publication, or the date it was notified to the pursuer or the date he became aware of it. This two month time limit is extended to take account of the distance of the applicant from the Court in Luxembourg. A 10 day extension applies to the United Kingdom. However, in exceptional circumstances, the applicant may be granted an extension, for example in the case of force majeure (*Bayer* [1994]).

Both legislative and non-legislative acts must be published in the Official Journal and enter into force on the day specified in the act or if this is not specified, on the 20th day following publication. Directives and decisions that specify to whom they are addressed only require to be notified to those addressees and come into force upon that notification.

If there is no challenge within the time limit, the measure is "good forever" and any challenge is inadmissible.

(5) What are the Consequences of Annulment?
Article 264 TFEU provides that if the action brought under art.263 TFEU is successful, the Court shall declare the measure void from the very beginning. The Court has no power to order the institution concerned to take any particular steps, but the institution is required under art.266 TFEU to take the measures necessary to comply with the Court's judgment and therefore to endeavour to recreate the situation which would have existed had the measure not been adopted.

If the measure is a regulation, only the offending parts may be annulled (art.264(2)) (*Société de Vente de Ciments et Bétons v Kerpen & Kerpen* [1983]); or the offending measure can remain in force until its replacement (*Timex v Council* [1985]); or, to preserve legal certainty, the annulment may only apply to the parties concerned in the case (*Simmenthal* [1979]).

ACTION AGAINST FAILURE OF AN INSTITUTION TO ACT UNDER ARTICLE 265 TFEU

Article 265 TFEU

"Should the European Parliament, the European Council, the Council, the Commission or the European Central Bank, in infringement of the Treaties, fail to act, the Member States and the other institutions of the Union may bring an action before the Court of Justice of the European Union to have the infringement established. This Article shall apply, under the same conditions, to bodies, offices and agencies of the Union which fail to act. The action shall be admissible only if the institution, body, office or agency concerned has first been called upon to act. If, within two months of being so called upon, the institution, body, office or agency concerned has not defined its position, the action may be brought within a further period of two months. Any natural or legal person may, under the conditions laid down in the preceding paragraphs, complain to the Court that an institution, body, office or agency of the Union has failed to address to that person any act other than a recommendation or an opinion."

(1) What may be Challenged?
Actions under art.265 TFEU can be regarded as "the other side of the coin" from actions under art.263 TFEU. While judicial review under art.263 TFEU may annul acts of the institutions, failure to act under art.265 TFEU may be used to compel an institution to fulfil its Union obligations. An action will thus *only be available where the applicant can show that such an obligation exists.*

Under the "unity principle" the Court has stated that "both provisions merely prescribe one and the same method of recourse" (*Chevalley v Commission* [1970]).

(2) Who has the Right to Challenge?
As with art.263 TFEU, there is a distinction between the status of applicants, with the applicants being either privileged, semi-privileged or non-privileged. Individuals may only challenge a failure to act when it concerns a binding act of which they would have been the addressee (*Mackprang v Commission* [1971]) and in which they are able to establish direct and individual concern, or direct concern only in the case of a regulatory act that does not entail implementing measures (*ENU v Commission* [1993]).

(3) What are the Relevant Time Limits?
Although the Treaty does not specify any time limit during which an action must be initiated, the applicant must approach the institution concerned beforehand and make it quite clear that if, within a two month time limit, it does not comply with its Union obligations to act, it will be subject to a

challenge under art.265 TFEU. Once this approach has been made the institution concerned has a period of two months within which to define its position. Most cases will be closed at this stage. If the institution does not define its position, the applicant has a further two months within which to bring the action.

(4) What are the Consequences of a Successful Challenge?
If the application under art.265 TFEU is upheld, the Court will declare that the failure to act is contrary to the Treaty and art.266 TFEU requires that the institution must, "take the necessary measures to comply with the judgment of the Court of Justice" within a reasonable period of time, in addition to any applicable requirement to make good damage under art.340 TFEU. If, however, the institution has defined its position but not adopted the disputed measure, it is not possible to bring an action for "failure to act" (*Lütticke* [1966]).

PLEA OF ILLEGALITY UNDER ARTICLE 277 TFEU

Article 277 TFEU

"Notwithstanding the expiry of the period laid down in Article 263, sixth paragraph, any party may, in proceedings in which an act of general application adopted by an institution, body, office or agency of the Union is at issue, plead the grounds specified in Article 263, second paragraph, in order to invoke before the Court of Justice of the European Union the inapplicability of that act."

This Treaty article also provides for a challenge to the act of an institution, in this case, a regulation. Unlike arts 263 and 265, a plea of illegality under art.277 is an indirect action. It is only available as a defence where other proceedings have been brought against the applicant and may be pleaded only in the course of proceedings which are already underway on other grounds (*Inuit Tapiriit Kanatami* [2013]). Because of the (still) restrictive nature of locus standi for the action of annulment under art.263 TFEU, individuals may not be able to mount a direct challenge to a legislative Regulation. However, in the course of art.263 TFEU proceedings challenging a decision, provided he overcomes the admissibility hurdle, he may claim that the original Regulation on which the decision is based, is illegal. This action has also been held to covers acts of the institutions which produce similar effects to those of regulations but which do not actually take the form of regulations (*Simmenthal* [1979]).

If the art.277 TFEU plea succeeds, although the regulation itself will not be annulled, its basis for the decision in question will be "inapplicable" and the decision will be void.

8. PRELIMINARY RULINGS

Giving effect to European Union law as set out by the Treaties and ensuring its provisions would be applied throughout the Member States by all national courts in a uniform and consistent manner was essential to the authors of the Union Treaties if the proper functioning of the internal market was to be achieved and preserved. To that end, art.19(3)(b) TEU and art.267 TFEU enable national courts and tribunals to refer questions of European Union law that require to be decided in a case pending before them to the Court of Justice of the European Union for a ruling. In the future, the General Court may be granted jurisdiction over certain art.267 actions, via amendments to the Statute of the Court of Justice (art.256(3) TFEU). This procedure has also proved to be the springboard for the development of some of the most fundamental concepts of Union law, such as direct effect and supremacy.

Notwithstanding the advances made for the benefit of individuals seeking to enforce their Union rights within their own national courts through the doctrine of direct effect, the preliminary ruling procedure has allowed them to mount challenges to the validity of Union acts in a manner which is much less restrictive than the procedural requirements of judicial review.

This preliminary rulings procedure is not one which an individual may use to bring his case direct. It is an "indirect action". It involves the national court hearing a case concerning a point of Union law and asking for guidance on its interpretation from the Court of Justice. The system of preliminary rulings represents a dialogue between a national court and the Court of Justice. The parties in the case cannot compel a national judge to make a request for a preliminary ruling to Luxembourg.

The procedure involves a national court seeking guidance on a point of interpretation, or validity of European law by formulating a question (or questions) for clarification by the Court of Justice (*Public Relations Consultants* [2013]). The case in the national court is then suspended until a ruling is given. The Court of Justice does not investigate the facts of the case, nor does it apply the law to the case (*Sandström* [2010]). It simply clarifies the point of European law. The judgment is binding on the national court referring the question which then continues the case and in due course, gives judgment in the light of the Court of Justice's interpretation of the law.

Article 267 itself provides a great deal of information on who may use it and when questions should be referred. It reads as follows:

"The Court of Justice of the European Union shall have jurisdiction to give preliminary rulings concerning:

(a) the interpretation of the Treaties;
(b) the validity and interpretation of acts of the institutions, bodies, offices or agencies of the Union;

Where such a question is raised before any court or tribunal of a
Member State, that court or tribunal may, if it considers that a decision
on the question is necessary to enable it to give judgment, request the
Court to give a ruling thereon.

Where any such question is raised in a case pending before a court or
tribunal of a Member State against whose decisions there is no
judicial remedy under national law, that court or tribunal shall bring
the matter before the Court.

If such a question is raised in a case pending before a court or tribunal
of a Member State with regard to a person in custody, the Court of
Justice of the European Union shall act with the minimum of delay."

The power of the Court therefore falls into two main groups—first is the
Court's interpretation of Union law and second is its power to rule on the
validity of the acts of the institutions. Note that in common with other
constitutional courts, the Court of Justice does not have the power to call
into question the validity of the founding constitutional texts, in this case
the Functioning Treaty, the Treaty of the European Union and the Euratom
Treaty.

THE INTERPRETATION OF EUROPEAN UNION LAW

Under art.267(1), the Court of Justice of the European Union has
jurisdiction to interpret:

- the Treaties;
- all the Acts of the EU institutions, bodies, office and agencies
  whether legally binding or not; and
- international agreements which are concluded by the Union with
  third countries.

Significantly, post Lisbon, the Court has assumed the general power to issue
preliminary rulings on matters concerning the Area of Freedom, Security
and Justice, subject to a five-year transitional period.

The main interpretative techniques of the Court of Justice are contextual
and teleological. Though it always starts with the text of the Treaties and
places the object and purpose of the provision in question within its context
in relation to other provisions, the Court may also look at the general
scheme of the Treaties as a whole and at its broad policy objectives, even
though these are set out in very general terms in the main.

THE VALIDITY OF THE ACTS OF THE EU INSTITUTIONS, BODIES, OFFICES AND AGENCIES

According to the judgment in *Grad* [1970], national courts are empowered to submit to the European Court all questions regarding validity of all measures without distinction. The Court can therefore rule on the validity of regulations, directives, decisions, recommendations and opinions.

Although the wording of art.267(1) mentions "validity", art.263 governing the system of judicial review concerns "legality" and so with these two articles the Court has created a complete system of legal remedies to review all the acts of the institutions (*Les Verts v European Parliament* [1986]).

Unlike the four grounds of review under art.263, art.267 does not contain any restrictions as to grounds on which validity of Union acts may be contested (*International Fruit Co (No.3)* [1972]).

As opposed to the time limitation by which cases for judicial review may be lodged, questions of validity may be raised under art.267 at any time.

The finding of the Court through a preliminary ruling is binding on the parties to the case in the national courts, but if an act of an institution is declared invalid, it is normally retroactive as under art.263 from when the act was originally adopted. If it is declared invalid, it is invalid throughout the Union.

There is nothing in the wording of art.267 to say who may declare a Union act invalid. In the case of *Foto-Frost* [1987] the Court stated that national courts may consider the validity of a Union act. If it is clearly valid, they may make a statement to this effect, though a national court cannot declare a Union act to be invalid. As a requirement of legal certainty, this is a prerogative of the Court of Justice which it will exercise through the preliminary ruling procedure.

Article 267(2) contains the provision for an optional or discretionary reference to the Court of Justice. When a matter comes before a national court it may refer a question though it is not obliged to do so (*Loss Relief Group Litigation Order* [2013]; and *Petition for Judicial Review by the Scotch Whisky Association* [2013]).

The national court must therefore establish the facts of the case before it. If an issue of Union law is critical to its final determination of the case and it does not have complete confidence in its ability to resolve the issue itself, it should refer the question to the Court of Justice. It should bear in mind the differences between national and Union legislation, the need for uniform interpretation throughout the Union and of the great advantages enjoyed by the Court of Justice in construing Union measures (*R v International Stock Exchanges, Ex p. Else* [1993]).

The Court of Justice does not enquire into the reasons why the national court has made a reference (*Costa v ENEL*), but the Court will not hear cases in which there is no real dispute between the parties, nor will it answer purely hypothetical questions (*Foglia v Novello* [1980]; *Schulte* [2005]).

If it were to do this, it would jeopardise the whole purpose of art.267. The Court may also reformulate the question posed.

As a matter of Union law, national courts have an absolute and unfettered discretion to refer which cannot be removed (*Auroux* [2007]). Thus any attempt to influence the Courts in this matter by Parliament or government would be unlawful.

By contrast, art.267(3) provides for a compulsory reference. The difference in the two paragraphs hinges on the words "may" and "shall". "May" means it is optional, at the discretion of the national court and "shall" conveys the imperative.

With a compulsory reference, the key words are "a court against whose decisions there is no judicial remedy". In these cases, if a question of Union law—interpretation or validity of a measure—is raised before a court from which there is no appeal, then that court is bound to send a question to the European Court (*Condron* [2010]). Failure of a national court to do so will invoke the liability of the Member State (*Köbler* [2003]; *Traghetti* [2006]; *Cooper* [2010]). The purpose of this goes to the heart of art.267. It will avoid a mistaken interpretation of Union law being given by the highest courts in the land, with other courts being bound by that decision through the doctrine of precedent. In other words, it prevents a body of national case law coming into existence in any Member State which is not in accordance with Union law. And, as with the whole of art.267, it ensures the uniform interpretation and application of the law.

A compulsory referral from a court from which there is no appeal also ensures that if a lower court has not made a reference to the Court of Justice—which it is perfectly entitled to do under art.267(2)—this is the final stage where any errors of law can be corrected.

So which actual courts in a Member State are subject to the obligation to refer? The problems which have arisen in this respect have led to the development of two theories:

(1) Only national courts which are always a court of last resort in the hierarchy of judicial precedent. For example, in Scotland the Supreme Court of the United Kingdom for civil matters and issues concerning devolution powers and the High Court of Justiciary for criminal cases. This is the abstract theory.
(2) The Court of Appeal in England, or in exceptional circumstances in the Scottish Court of Session when leave to appeal to the Supreme Court has been refused. This is known as the concrete theory (see *R v Henn and Derby* [1979]; *Lyckeskog* [2002]).

Article 267(2) also mentions the words "any court or tribunal". When is a body a court or tribunal, and when is it not? Cases have come to the European Court from quasi-judicial bodies and the question was to establish their locus standi—whether or not they were allowed even to refer a case to the Court of Justice.

Courts of law within the judicial hierarchy of a Member State have automatic status. Whether other bodies, such as arbitration tribunals and appeals committees, for example, had locus standi was more problematic. In the case of *Walter Schmid* [2002] the Court of Justice set out the essential characteristics of a "court or tribunal" within the Union context. The criteria to be used to measure whether this was so were that the body:

- is established by law;
- is permanent;
- has compulsory jurisdiction;
- its procedure is inter pares;
- applies the rule of law; and
- is independent.

The right to refer questions to the Court of Justice belongs to national "courts or tribunals" only. Parliaments, governments and Union institutions do not have locus standi to submit questions for preliminary rulings.

As stated earlier, art.267(3) lays down an obligatory referral in cases where there "is no judicial remedy". National supreme courts are understandably reluctant to constantly refer questions on issues where they believe the European Court has already clarified the point (*OFT v Abbey National* [2009]; and *Russell v Transocean International Resources* [2011]). The Court of Justice itself has recognised that there may be occasions where it is not necessary to make a preliminary ruling. This relaxation of the strict nature of art.267(3) is based on French administrative law. It means that no question of interpretation is necessary where a provision is quite clear. The Court described the circumstances in which a national court of last resort need not refer a question in the case of *CILFIT* [1982]:

- where a question of Union law is irrelevant to the case at issue;
- the point has already been decided by a previous decision of the Court of Justice (the doctrine of acte éclairé);
- if the correct application of Union law is so obvious as to leave no doubt as to the manner in which the matter is to be resolved (the doctrine of acte clair); and
- the matter is equally obvious to the Courts of the other Member States and to the Court of Justice.

The Court went on to set out the problems were a national supreme court to decide not to ask for a preliminary ruling in these circumstances:

- European Union law is drafted in several different languages all of them equally authentic and binding, so any interpretation by a national court would require a comparison of all different language versions.
- Union law has its own particular terminology, such that legal concepts do not necessarily have the same meaning in Union law as

they do in national law.
- Union law must always be interpreted in context and in the light of the purposes of the treaties as a whole, of the objectives of Union law and the evolution of Union law at that particular time, in other words, interpretation is by the teleological method.

Now that Union law is becoming more and more familiar to national judges, it is not unusual for the national supreme courts to use the doctrine of *acte clair* and decide cases containing a point of Union law without referring to the Court in Luxembourg (*British Fuels v Baxendale* [1999]; and *OFT v Abbey National* [2009]).

To ensure that national courts are fully aware of the circumstances and the manner in which references should be made under art.267, the Court of Justice is empowered to issue guidance notes and recommendations. The most recent recommendation notice was issued in November 2012, (2012/C 338/01).

In addition, the Rules of Procedure of the Court of Justice have been amended in order to simplify the procedure for cases in which questions referred by a national court are identical to questions that have already been answered, where the answer to the question can be clearly deduced from existing case law or where the answer admits of no reasonable doubt. In these cases, the Court of Justice may give its decision by reasoned order. It may also:

- request from the parties all such information relating to the facts and any other relevant documents; and
- request clarification from national courts which refer questions to it for a preliminary ruling.

The deepening and widening of European integration inevitably took its toll on the efficiency of the Court of Justice, such that art.267 actions were accompanied by significant delay. To address this bottleneck, the Court set up an expedited or accelerated procedure whereby, if a matter is considered to be of exceptional urgency, the Court can restrict the matters requiring a ruling to essential points of law, thus speeding up the response time.

Further, since 2008, in relation to the Area of Freedom, Security and Justice, the Court has had the power to hear a case under the urgent procedure, known by its French acronym PPU (*Detiček* [2009]; *Kadzoev* [2009]; *Leymann and Pustovarov* [2008]; *McB* [2010]; *El Dridi* [2011] and *West* [2012]). This procedural amendment has been augmented by art.267(4) TFEU. This subparagraph explicitly provides that the Court must act swiftly if the preliminary ruling is required in connection with a national case where a party is in custody.

The effect of a preliminary ruling is to bind the national court in the case in which the reference was made and any other national court considering the same point of law.

The preliminary rulings procedure:

- gives individuals the opportunity for an indirect challenge to the validity of Union law within their own national courts;
- allows an individual to obtain domestic remedies which would otherwise not be available in the event of a direct challenge under art.263;
- is a Court-to-Court dialogue only;
- provides guidance to a national court when applying the law;
- is not an appeals procedure;
- allows Union law to be interpreted by one authoritative source in a consistent and uniform manner throughout all Member States;
- has allowed the Court of Justice of the European Union to extend the scope and effectiveness of the Union legal order;
- is not limited to the four grounds of review essential under art.263;
- may be raised by a national court at any time;
- must be raised by a national court or tribunal (within the Union context) unless the national court applies the *acte clair* doctrine; and
- binds the court or tribunal which made the reference to the Court of Justice.

9. THE AREA OF FREEDOM, SECURITY AND JUSTICE

European integration, although essentially economic in nature, has always impliedly encompassed the idea of safety, justice and security. The internal market was always envisaged as a precursor to further, deeper integration for the Member States. In addition, it was recognised that further liberalisation in relation to European free movement would need to be accompanied by corresponding measures to ensure that the internal market did not result in increased criminality. In 1975 the Trevi group was set up to tackle the threat posed to economic prosperity posed by terrorism. Its remit was widened to counter trafficking in drugs and arms a decade later in 1985.

At the same time of course, certain member States, namely the Benelux countries, France and Germany, were working together on measures to abolish their internal borders through the intergovernmental Schengen Agreement, with the Schengen Convention of 1990 giving effect to the 1985 agreement and coming into force in 1995. This agreement is designed to abolish internal border controls between its Member States and to provide for improved external border controls, to compensate for increased internal liberalisation.

The development of these disparate, although connected, initiatives led to calls for the incorporation of such measures into the European Community legal system and for a system of recognition for de facto forms of increased integration. However, since these measures were highly politically sensitive and seen as central to a Member State's sense of sovereignty, the idea of pooling resources under a supranational legal system was not enthusiastically welcomed. Agreement could only be secured on a weaker form of intergovernmental cooperation for action in the fields of foreign and security policy and justice and home affairs and limited scope for engaging in closer cooperation. Thus the three pillar structure of Maastricht was born.

Once the legal structure of Maastricht had been agreed upon and progress on Schengen cooperation was taking shape, the Member States were emboldened to take further action in rationalising developments in this fledgling area. Significantly, the concept of an Area of Freedom, Security and Justice was first introduced into EU law by the Treaty of Amsterdam and Amsterdam also brought the Schengen Convention into the EU legal structure (*Gözütok and Brügge* [2003]). This concept straddled the three pillars of the European Union and was designed to counter the perception that the free movement rights of the EU's internal market and the abolition of internal border checks could become a criminal's charter. The economic freedoms of the Treaty were not to result in increased cross-border crime and reduced cross-border cooperation. Also, action in this area must respect and build upon the *acquis communitaire* of the European Union. The Tampere programme of October 1999 set out the first five year plan for the Area of Freedom, Security and Justice. One of the most significant achievements of this programme was the promulgation of the Framework Decision on the European Arrest Warrant (*Constantin Sandi v The Craiova Court, Romania* [2009]).

In turn, this programme was replaced by the Hague Programme which ran until the end of 2009. The third, and most recent, five year roadmap was laid out in the Stockholm Programme, "An open and secure Europe serving and protecting citizens" (O.J. [2010] C 115/1).

In parallel, in order to bridge the gap between the first and third pillars, the Treaty of Amsterdam formalised the general rules for engaging in closer cooperation and brought a significant number of justice and home affairs issue into the first pillar of the European Union. The Treaty of Nice renamed the closer cooperation procedure as enhanced cooperation and the Lisbon Treaty now requires that at least nine Member States be involved in establishing enhanced cooperation (art.20.2 TEU).

The Lisbon Treaty abolished the three pillar structure, paving the way for more coherent and consistent action in these policy fields. The Area of Freedom, Security and Justice now comprises an area without internal frontiers, which ensures the free movement of persons, whilst outlining measures as to external border controls, asylum, immigration and the prevention and combating of crime (art.3(2) TEU). The power of the EU to take action in this field is limited by the principle of proportionality since the AFSJ is a shared competence (art.4(2)(j) TFEU). Nevertheless, the European Council has a wide discretion when deciding upon the most appropriate measures to give effect to the area of freedom, security and justice (*Advocaten voor de Wereld* [2007]).

After the Treaty of Lisbon, action under the Area of Freedom, Security and Justice encompasses the following policy areas (Title V, arts 67–89 TFEU):

- action to underpin the Schengen area principles;
- the free movement of persons and citizenship, including action on visa, immigration and asylum policy and the protection of fundamental rights and data protection;
- action to prevent crime, particularly organised crime, sexual offences, racism, xenophobia and terrorism and to coordinate drugs policy;
- to provide for an EU external borders and external relations policy, including provisions on enlargement of the EU; and
- administrative cooperation between the police, customs and the European judiciary (in both civil and criminal matters).

The concept of EU citizenship and the accompanying economic and non-economic freedoms is the predominant limb of the Area of Freedom, Security and Justice and is the area that has seen greatest development (see Ch.11). Concrete agreements in Security and Justice have proven more difficult to achieve, partly because of their previously inter-governmental nature. Additionally, even though the Lisbon Treaty abolishes the three pillar structure and incorporates the second and third pillars into the European Union structure, Member States are entitled to continue to opt-out of certain measures in this field. Thus, Ireland, the United Kingdom and Denmark participate to a greater or lesser extent in this area (*United Kingdom v Council*, [2008] Cases C-137/05 and C-77/05). A further impediment to full compliance with AFSJ rules is that, notwithstanding the coming into force of Lisbon, the Court of Justice does not have jurisdiction to review the validity or proportionality of actions of national police or law-enforcement in relation to maintaining law and order and internal security (art.276 TFEU) and all other areas of police and criminal justice only come under the jurisdictional ambit of the Court of Justice on December 1, 2014. By the end of May of that year, the UK Government must decide on whether to continue to be bound by all of these legislative measures or whether to opt-in to selected police and criminal justice measures on an ad-hoc basis.

THE SCHENGEN ACQUIS

The Schengen Agreement applies to all EU member States with the exception of Ireland and the United Kingdom, by virtue of their opt-out Bulgaria and Romania, due to their lack of preparedness in complying with the Schengen acquis, Cyprus because of the Turkish presence in the north of the island and Croatia by dint of its recent accession. Croatia is expected to join Schengen in 2015. In addition, the Schengen rules apply in four non-EU states, namely, Iceland, Lichtenstein, Norway and Switzerland. Primarily, Schengen provides for the abolition of checks on persons at the internal borders and a corresponding strengthening of the common external border controls, through the introduction of a Schengen Borders Code (Regulation 562/2006 as variously amended; *Zurita García* [2009]). In order to achieve these objectives, Schengen harmonises the conditions of entry and the rules on visas and provides for police and judicial cooperation. The police are able to conduct surveillance operations across the Schengen territory and engage in "hot" pursuit of suspects and criminals. The Schengen system, in order to work effectively, relies on accurate and up to date information sharing between the Member States. This is guaranteed through the Schengen Information System (SIS II as established by Regulation 2424/2001, as amended). Monitoring and management of the EU's external borders, by the Member States, is facilitated by Frontex, the EU's border agency (Regulation 2007/2004, as amended). Further, the EU is committed to the creation of an Integrated Border Management System.

CITIZENSHIP, ASYLUM, FUNDAMENTAL RIGHTS
AND DATA PROTECTION

European Union citizenship offers a number of significant rights to Member State nationals, concerning free movement, participation in the political life of the EU and procedural safeguards (see the chapter on citizenship).

The systematic persecution of human beings across the globe has given rise to a massive influx of people seeking protection in the European Union. As a response to this situation, the European Union has taken concrete steps to establish a Common European Asylum System. This system consists of a number of laws designed to streamline the process of applying for European asylum and protection. The Dublin Regulation 343/2000 outlines the rules applicable for determining the Member State responsible for examining an asylum application. These rules are designed to bolster the free movement of persons through limiting the scope for third country nationals to engage in forum shopping as regards asylum applications (*R (on the application of S) v Home Secretary* [2010]). Uniformity of interpretation as to who is to be offered EU protection is provided for by the recast Qualification Directive 2011/95 (*Elgafaji v Staatssecretaris van Justitie* [2009]; *Abdulla* [2010]), whilst the Reception Directive 2003/9, the Asylum Procedures Directive 2005/85 and the Temporary Protection Directive 2001/55 set out the minimum standards of treatment and rights to be enjoyed by asylum seekers and refugees. Underpinning this system is the Eurodac Regulation, which requires Member States to identify asylum seekers and refugees through fingerprinting (Regulations 2725/2000 and 407/2002), and Regulation 439/2010, establishing the European Asylum Support Office.

Taken together, these rules are designed to give practical effect to the Geneva Convention on Refugees 1951, the jus cogens principle of *non-refoulement*, or non-return and the right to asylum as expressed in art.18 of the Charter of Fundamental Rights (*QD and AH (Iraq) v Home Secretary* [2009]). Nevertheless, concerns remain about the EU Asylum regime and its compliance with the European Convention of Human Rights (*M.S.S. v Belgium and Greece* [2011]; *N.S. v Secretary of State for the Home Department* [2011]).

Further consolidation in this field, in order to complete the Common European Asylum System, was expected to be completed by 2012 but has been pushed backwards towards the end of 2013 and into 2014.

Fundamental rights are an integral part of EU activities. The Union protects fundamental rights as general principles of EU law, as principles common to the laws of the Member States and as specific enumerated rights of the Charter of Fundamental Rights. Oversight of the EU's effectiveness in protecting and securing fundamental rights is provided by the EU's Fundamental Rights Agency (Regulation 168/2007).

Data protection is a major concern for the European Union and the EU has been at the forefront of developments in this field. The EU has enacted generic data protection laws (Data Protection Directive 95/46), as well as sector specific laws, designed to deal with issues as diverse as electronic communications (E-Privacy Directive 2002/58), the interception of communications (Data Retention Directive 2006/24) and protection within the framework of police and judicial co-operation in criminal matters (Framework Decision 2008/977). The EU institutions themselves are bound by data protection rules (Regulation 45/2001). Oversight of data protection laws is provided through the European Data Protection Supervisor and guidance on best practice is promulgated by the art.29, Working Party on Data Protection. Significant strengthening of the significance of Data Protection to the European Union legal system was secured by the Treaty of Lisbon. Data Protection was elevated to the status of primary law through art.16 TFEU and is also protected via art.8 of the Charter of Fundamental Rights. Notwithstanding these improvements, the Commission, in 2012, proposed a radical overhaul of Directive 95/46 in order to take account of technological developments.

CRIME

Alongside measures to promote general mutual recognition of the (diverse) Member States' criminal law systems, the European Union has been prolific in harmonising substantive criminal law. In the past such harmonising measures were undertaken by way of Framework Decisions enacted under the third pillar and related to serious cross border crimes, such as trafficking in human beings, drugs (Framework Decision 2004/757) and arms; the sexual exploitation of children; terrorism (Framework Decisions 2008/919 and 2002/475); financial crime, such as money laundering (Framework Decision 2001/500), counterfeiting and fraud (Framework Decisions 2001/413, 2001/888 and 2000/383); computer crime (Framework Decision 2005/222); organised crime (Framework Decision 2008/841); and racism and xenophobia (Framework Decision 2008/913). Over time, these framework decisions may be repealed and replaced by harmonising directives enacted under art.83 TFEU. To date, in exercise of this new power, the European Union has enacted harmonising directives on combating the sexual abuse and exploitation of children (Directive 2011/92) and on human trafficking (Directive 2011/36) and submitted a proposal for a directive on cybercrime (COM (2010) 517). The Council is expected to approve this cybercrime directive by the end of 2013.

The victims of crime benefit from harmonised rules as to compensation, as set out in Directive 2004/80, and to recognition within the criminal legal system, as per Directive 2012/29. However, the concept of "victim" does not extend to legal persons (*Dell'Orto* [2007]; Directive 2012/29).

COOPERATION

The intergovernmental origins of action to provide for security and justice necessarily means that action in this field has been predicated upon coordination of Member State action and mutual recognition of that action. This emphasis upon mutual recognition subsists post Lisbon.

Law enforcement cooperation is assured via Europol and CEPOL. In order to combat cross-border serious crime, Europol, the European Law Enforcement Agency, was established to support and strengthen mutual cooperation between the Member States' police authorities and other law enforcement services (art.88 TFEU and Decision 2009/371/JHA). CEPOL is the European Police College and provides training for senior police officers throughout the European Union, alongside facilitating cooperative networks between the national training centres (Decision 2005/681/JHA).

Eurojust is the European Union's judicial cooperation unit and comprises 28 members, drawn from each Member State, who are judges, prosecutors or police officers (Decision 2002/187/JHA as amended). Eurojust is designed to assist in the fight against serious crime, through facilitating cooperation in the investigation and prosecution processes. In particular, it improves cooperation between the competent authorities of the Member States by facilitating the execution of international mutual legal assistance and the implementation of extradition and transfer requests. At a more practical level, contact between national courts is coordinated through the European Judicial Network as regards civil, commercial and criminal matters (Decision 2008/976/JHA, Decision 2001/470/EC and Decision 568/2009/EC).

Article 86 TFEU empowers the Union, in the future, to establish a European Public Prosecutor's Office as an adjunct to Eurojust. Such an organisation would be given the mandate to investigate and prosecute crimes that affect the Union's financial interests and is designed to complement the work of the European Anti-Fraud Office ("OLAF").

Judicial cooperation in criminal matters is dominated by the development of the European Arrest Warrant system. The creation of a single travel zone required that extradition be abolished and replaced with a faster system of surrender for accused persons and prisoners (*Wolzenburg* [2010]), alongside more efficient enforcement of criminal judgments. Thus, the European Arrest Warrant was created in 2002 (*Asztaslos* [2010]). The European arrest warrant is predicated upon the mutual recognition of the criminal law systems of the member States, which in itself presupposes a high level of mutual trust and respect for the national systems (*Armas* [2005]; *Assange v Sweden* [2012]). The European Arrest Warrant has proved to be a highly contentious area of EU law, raising issues of constitutional importance, such as the supremacy of the system (*Constitutionality of Framework Decision on the European Arrest Warrant, Re* [2007]) and of interpretative difficulty, in particular in relation to the principle of *ne bis in idem* (the right not to be tried or punished twice, that is double jeopardy) (*Turanský* [2009]) and the extent to which a national court may decline to execute a European Arrest Warrant. It is clear that only in exceptional cases, would it ever be permissible to refuse to execute a European arrest warrant and the pursuer in such a case would have to discharge the exacting onus of proof that the requesting Member State's legal system is defective (*Engler v Lord Advocate* [2010]; and *Trajer v HMA* [2009]).

Allied to this system is the introduction of the European Evidence Warrant (Framework Decision 2008/978). This Framework Decision simplifies the procedure for Member States' judges and public prosecutors obtaining evidence from other Member States, for use in a criminal trial. The Decision builds upon Framework Decision 2003/577 on the execution of orders freezing property and evidence.

A lynchpin of judicial cooperation is that the courts of the Member States must be able to take account of judgments rendered by other national courts. To this end, in the criminal law sphere, the European Union has legislated to provide for the mutual recognition of financial penalties (Council Framework Decision 2005/214), measures of supervision rendered as alternatives to pre-trial detention (Framework Decision 2009/829), court sanctioned protective measures (Directive 2011/99) and has empowered national courts to be able to take into account previous convictions rendered in other Member States (Framework Decision 2008/675). Further action in this field encompasses provisions providing for the harmonisation of procedural rights of the defence and the issue of *in absentia* judgments (Framework Decision 2009/299), as well as measures to deal with the assumption of jurisdiction by national courts (Framework Decision 2009/948).

In terms of judicial cooperation in civil matters, significant work has been achieved in terms of private international law, in regard to conflict of laws and jurisdiction. The Rome I Regulation 593/2008 and the Rome II Regulation 864/2007 set out the rules on the law applying to contractual obligations and non-contractual (that is, delictual) obligations respectively. Essentially, these regulations provide for the law to apply to the dispute be that of the law agreed upon by the parties to the contract or where the harmful event took place, subject to certain tightly defined exceptions. The Rome III Regulation 1259/2010 is an example of enhanced cooperation and applies to cases of divorce and legal separation for participating member states only. Under the jurisdictional rules of the Brussels I Regulation 44/2001, the defender to the action is generally to be sued in his country of domicile, except in relation to cases of special or exclusive jurisdiction, such as in cases of consumer contracts and immovable property disputes (*Rehder v Air Baltic Corporation* [2009]). Thus, for example, in relation to consumer contracts, the consumer can raise an action against the defender in his country of domicile rather than having to sue the defender in their home state and the law applicable to the dispute will be the law of the consumer's home state. In disputes concerning immovable property, the courts of the country where the property is situated will have jurisdiction. Again, agreement may oust these jurisdictional presumptions and, jurisdiction may be claimed by a national court where a defender did not object to the jurisdiction of that court and indeed made an appearance before that court (*Bilas* [2010]). In light of the increasing complexity of this area of law, the Brussels I Regulation will be superseded by the recast regulation on jurisdiction and recognition and enforcement of judgments in January 2015 (Regulation 1215/2012).

As more cross-border family inter-relationships are created, and thereafter dissolve, across Europe, the European Union needed to enact laws securing family law obligations. Therefore, the EU enacted the

Brussels II Regulation (Regulation 2201/2003; *Proceedings brought by A* [2010]). This regulation applies to matrimonial issues and those of parental responsibility. In general, the courts of the State where the child or spouses have their habitual residence will have jurisdiction, again subject to defined exceptions to that rule.

10. CITIZENSHIP AND THE FREE MOVEMENT OF PERSONS

The concept of citizenship was introduced into EU law by the Maastricht Treaty and is now principally found in arts 20–25 TFEU and in the Charter of Fundamental Rights. Originally, these provisions were considered to be merely exhortatory, adding nothing of substance to the range of rights granted under the EU Treaties. Indeed, the original concept of free movement was predicated upon the existence of an economic rationale for the move, such that the Member State national was either a worker, self-employed provider of services or a recipient of services. However, the notion of "European citizenship" has been progressively interpreted by the Court of Justice of the European Union, such that it now offers autonomous rights for European individuals, independently of the other substantive rights set out in the EU Treaties.

Article 20 TFEU sets out that:

> "Citizenship of the Union is hereby established. Every person holding the nationality of a Member State shall be a citizen of the Union. Citizenship of the Union shall be additional to and not replace national citizenship."

Thus, acquisition of EU citizenship is not consistently obtained across the EU, being as it is dependent upon the national rules of each Member State granting nationality (*Kaur* [2001]). However, these autonomous national rules must respect EU law principles (*Rottmann* [2010]).

The Functioning Treaty sets out that citizenship confers four specific rights:

- to move freely and reside in the territory of Member States (art.21 TFEU and art.45 of the Charter);
- to vote and stand as a candidate in local and European Parliament elections in the Member State of residence (not of nationality) (art.22 TFEU and art.39 of the Charter; (*McGeogh v Lord President of the Council* [2011]);
- to protection, in a non-EU country in which the citizen's own Member State is not represented, by the diplomatic or consular authorities of any other Member State (art.23 TFEU and art.46 of the Charter); and
- to petition the European Parliament and to apply to the European Ombudsman and to receive a reply in the citizen's own language (art.24 TFEU and art.41(4) of the Charter).

It is axiomatic that in order for certain aspects of EU citizenship law to be engaged, the EU citizen must be in a position to exercise their free movement rights (*McCarthy* [2011]; *Dereci* [2011]; and *Yoshikazu Iida* [2012]).

In addition, the Treaty on European Union provides that citizens are able to petition the Commission in order to request the Commission to draw up a new legislative proposal (art.11 TEU). This right of petition is engaged where at least 1 million citizens across at least seven Member States agree upon a proposal to be submitted to the Commission (art.24 TFEU and Regulation 211/2011). Citizens are also entitled to access EU documents (art.15(3) TFEU).

The original wording of the Treaty on European Union indicated that no new free movement rights for persons were to be brought into being, but solely attached the existing rights—with all their qualifications and derogations—to the new concept of citizenship. Although the exact rights of citizens were unclear, it was not long before cases arrived before the European Courts in which citizenship was a central issue:

- *Uecker and Jacquet* [1997]—citizenship was not intended to extend the scope of the Treaty to cover internal situations with no link to Union law.
- *Martinez Sala* [1998]—any Spanish national living in Germany not falling within the Union definition of "a worker" (i.e. not carrying out economic activity) and thus not falling within the personal scope of the legal provisions was still entitled to equal treatment in relation to welfare as she came within the material scope of these benefits.
- *Grzelczyk* [2001]—a French student in Belgium, again, not a "worker" in the Union sense and thus not entitled to benefits, was considered to have been discriminated against contrary to art.18 TFEU in conjunction with the Treaty provisions on citizenship. The Court explicitly stated in this case that Union citizenship is destined to be the fundamental status of nationals of the Member States.
- *Baumbast* [2002]—a citizen of the Union who no longer enjoyed a right of residence in a host Member State possessed a fundamental right to move and reside freely within the Union, subject to limitations and conditions laid down elsewhere in Union law. Such limitations must be exercised in accordance with the principle of proportionality, may not be arbitrary nor must they deprive the residence rights endowed of their substantive content.
- *Zhu and Chen* [2004]—A Chinese couple visited the United Kingdom. The wife gave birth to a daughter whilst in Belfast. The child gained Irish nationality and thus EU citizenship. Mrs Chen moved to Cardiff and sought residency for her family, which was denied. The Court of Justice stated that by virtue of art.21 (and applicable secondary legislation) parents could not be deprived of their right to reside with their child, who is a Union citizen.
- *Bidar* [2005]—Non-UK students from other member states must be able to become settled by reason of their lawful presence as a student in the United Kingdom, in order to then become eligible for student related financial assistance. The UK rules at the time made it impossible for a non-UK student to ever acquire settled status. The

Court of Justice held that the non-discrimination rules of art.18 TFEU applied to such a situation.

- *Förster* [2008]—Following on from *Bidar*, the Court of Justice agreed with the Netherlands that it could impose a five-year integration period before awarding student financial assistance.
- *Jipa* [2008]—European citizens have the right to leave their home State.
- *Huber* [2008]—a computerised system for fighting crime, which only processed the personal data of foreign nationals, violated the principle of non-discrimination.
- *Rottmann* [2010]—Mr Rottmann, an Austrian, acquired German nationality, by deception. The German authorities then deprived Mr Rottmann of this nationality and he had already lost his Austrian nationality. The Court held that EU law did not stop Germany from removing a grant of nationality, as long as such a measure was proportionate.
- *Bressol* [2010]—Limits on the number of non-resident students who can apply for medical training, may, very exceptionally, be justified as a necessary public health restriction on the free movement of citizens.
- *Zambrano* [2011]—A Colombian national could acquire a right to remain in Belgium, in order to ensure that his Belgian children could fully enjoy their citizenship rights under EU law, in particular the human right to enjoy a family life.
- *Prete* [2012]—The Court held that it was disproportionate for Belgium to refuse to allow EU students seeking their first job after graduation in Belgium an entitlement to a tideover financial allowance, on the basis that they had not studied in Belgium for the previous six years.
- *Byankov* [2012]—It was illegal for Bulgaria to prevent a Bulgarian national from leaving the country or renewing a passport on the basis of a failure to pay a pre-existing debt.

With the *Baumbast* case came the recognition by the Court that art.21 TFEU was directly effective and therefore could be relied on to provide autonomous rights which an individual could enforce through local courts. However, there was also a need to clarify the exact procedural and substantive rights that Union citizens possess by virtue of their status as Union citizens and as such Directive 2004/38 (The Citizenship Directive) was enacted.

The European Union considered that the best way to provide for autonomous citizenship rights would be to consolidate the disparate rules covering workers, self-employed people and service receivers and providers, and to progressively endow these rights on non-economically active EU nationals. Thus, to understand the law of EU citizenship, one must understand the historical underpinnings of (economic) free movement. Even today, notwithstanding the new citizenship provisions, it is still the case that being economically active is the best guarantee for a person being enabled to exercise their right of free movement under European law.

In the past, the free movement of people was mostly undertaken for the purpose of rebuilding Europe with cheap, temporary, manual labour. As such, full integration of the European continent would only be truly achieved if all economically active citizens were encouraged to move to other Member States' territories and were to do so for longer periods of time, including permanent migration. Thus, incentives would have to be provided to encourage the take up of these migratory rights, alongside the removal of barriers to free movement. Over time, rules were adopted on such things as, recognition of qualifications, as well as inducements for students to study abroad, the right to bring family members, the right to enter and remain on host State territory and extension of the concept of non-discrimination to services and benefits offered by the host Member State and finally the increasingly potent citizenship rights.

RIGHT OF EXIT, ENTRY AND RESIDENCE

Clearly, the right of entry to and residence in another Member State and the right to leave one's own state are of fundamental importance in securing the fundamental freedoms of the Treaty. Without these practical rights, free movement would be rendered nugatory. However, just as important for European integration is the right for EU citizens to install their family members with them in the host State.

Thus, Directive 2004/38 enumerates the following autonomous rights for Union citizens and their family members:

- To leave the territory of a Member State and to enter another Member State, subject to possession of a passport or valid identity card (art.4; *Yiadom* [2000]). Union citizens must be granted or be able to renew a passport or identity card. Non-EU family members must possess a valid passport.
- To enter another Member State upon presentation of a valid identity card or passport (art.5). Family members can enter with a valid passport. The host Member State may require an entry visa for third country national family members.
- To reside in the territory of the host Member State for up to three months without any conditions or formalities other than those applicable to possession of a valid passport or identity card, as applicable (art.6; *Baumbast* [2002]).
- To reside in the territory of the host Member State beyond three months where one of the following criteria is satisfied:

    (i)   The Union citizen is a worker or self-employed person in the host Member State.

    (ii)   The Union citizen and family members are not a burden on the social assistance system of the host Member State; that is they have "sufficient resources".

(iii) The Union citizen is enrolled on a course of study at a recognised educational establishment, has comprehensive sickness insurance and has sufficient resources to prevent him/her becoming a burden on the social assistance system of the host Member State.

(iv) However, more liberal rules apply where the Union citizen is a child, dependent upon a parent who is not a national of the host State (*Ibrahim and Teixeira* [2010]).

Citizens' Families

Article 2(2) of Directive 2004/38 defines what is meant by "members of a citizen's family" for the purpose of deciding who will be allowed to migrate with the citizen to the host state. These are:

- a citizen's spouse/partner (where national law treats registered partnerships and marriage as equivalent) and descendants who are under the age of 21 or are dependants, including those of the spouse/partner; and
- dependant relatives in the ascending line of the citizen and his/her spouse/partner.

In *Lebon* [1987], it was established that even if an adult child is over 21, if he or she is still dependant, then they are still regarded in law as members of the family and are entitled to claim Union family rights, although the onus is on the adult dependant to prove such dependency (*Bigia v Entry Clearance Officer* [2009]). The dependency is as a result of a factual situation, not derived from the national legislation of a host Member State.

Third country national spouses do not need to have previously lawfully resided in another Member State before exercising their parasitic right to free movement (*Metock* [2008]).

The extension of the family member rights to include partners in addition to spouses is a recognition of progressive case law developments in the area (*Reed* [1986]), which in themselves explicitly acknowledged the immense societal changes occurring within the European Union. If a married couple separates at any time, spouse's rights do not come to an end until they are divorced (*Diatta* [1985]).

By virtue of Directive 2004/38, this right extends to partners in a relationship analogous to marriage, where national law equates such relationships to a marriage. In the case of divorce or termination of partnership, the family member is now explicitly granted the right to remain in the host territory (art.13 of the directive). The directive does however make a distinction between family members who are EU nationals and those who have third country nationality. For ex-partners/spouses who possess a third country nationality, right to reside will depend upon the existence of a number of factors, such as sufficient length of the relationship, the custody and access situation as regards children of the marriage/relationship and the prior existence of "particularly difficult circumstances", such as domestic violence.

As stated earlier, members of a citizen's family are entitled to migrate with the EU citizen regardless of their own nationality—though of course the EU citizen, whom they are parasitic upon, must be a national of another Member State exercising their right of free movement, by crossing a border (*Morson and Jhabjan v the Netherlands* [1982]). These qualifying family members have the right to reside and to take up any employment throughout the territory of that same state even if they are not nationals of any Member State of the Union (art.23 of Directive 2004/38).

In the case of residence beyond three months, the directive permits Member States to impose certain registration formalities upon the Union citizen and his/her family members (arts 8 and 9). In particular, the host Member State must provide for registration to be open for at least three months after arrival. Thereupon, a registration certificate must be issued, in the situation where the Union citizen presents a valid identity card or passport and proof of either employment/self-employment, proof of sufficient resources and appropriate sickness insurance, or proof of enrolment on an approved course of study, sufficient resources and appropriate sickness insurance. In the case of EU national family members, a residence certificate will be issued upon presentation of a valid identity card or passport and documentary evidence of the relevant family relationship. Non-EU national family members must comply with the requirements of arts 9–11. The third country family members must apply for a residence card, which will be issued upon presentation of the family member's passport, official evidence of the family relationship and the registration certificate of the Union citizen. The residence card must be valid for at least five years. A failure to comply with formalities regarding entry and residence cannot justify a deportation order. Any such applicable sanctions for non-compliance must be non-discriminatory and proportionate (arts 8(2) and 9(3) of Directive 2004/38; *R v Pieck* [1980]; *Royer* [1977]; *Watson and Belmann* [1976]).

The free movement of workers still constitutes one of the cornerstones of the internal market. An extensive system of Treaty provisions, secondary legislation and the case law of the Court provides for a system of employment rights throughout the Union prohibiting national legislation which might place other Union nationals at a disadvantage when they seek to exercise their right of free movement. Notwithstanding the vast corpus of law, guidance and information available, workers still experience problems in fully exercising their rights, thus justifying periodic legislative intervention ("Commission Proposal for a Directive on measures facilitating the exercise of rights conferred on workers" [2013] (COM (2013) 236 final).

The basic principle covering these rights is that of non-discrimination of persons from other Member States on the grounds of nationality as set out in art.18 TFEU and art.21 of the Charter. This principle is incorporated within all the other provisions in this area either through the Treaties, in the secondary legislation or through the case law of the Court.

Among the provisions promoting free movement of workers are the following:

- Article 45 TFEU defines what is meant by free movement of workers. This is considered in detail below.
- Article 46 TFEU relates to the implementation of art.45 TFEU by setting out the legislative manner in which the goal of free movement may be achieved. It relates to close co-operation between national employment services, abolishing restrictions and by setting up appropriate machinery, "to bring offers of employment into touch with applications for employment and to facilitate the achievement of a balance between supply and demand in the employment market in such a way as to avoid serious threats to the standard of living and level of employment in the various regions and industries".
- Article 47 TFEU provides for the exchange of young workers.
- Article 48 TFEU relates to social security in relation to the free movement of workers.
- Article 18 TFEU provides a general prohibition of discrimination on the grounds of nationality.
- Article 157 TFEU on equal pay for equal work.
- Article 19 TFEU authorises the Council and the Parliament to take legislative action to combat discrimination based on sex, racial or ethnic origin, religion or belief, disability, age or sexual orientation.

Several major pieces of secondary legislation also facilitated those falling within their personal scope to exercise their right of free movement. Unfortunately, the fact that there was such a volume of legislation governing this area meant that citizens were often unsure of their exact rights under the Treaties and the secondary legislation, such that they were discouraged from actually exercising these rights. Therefore, the Commission introduced Directive 2004/38 to consolidate the law in this area. The directive broadly repeals the secondary legislation, but a number of connected provisions are to be found in Regulation 492/2011.

Article 45 TFEU sets out that:

"(1) Freedom of movement for workers shall be secured within the Union.

(2) Such freedom of movement shall entail the abolition of any discrimination based on nationality between workers of the Member States as regards employment, remuneration and other conditions of work and employment.

(3) It shall entail the rights, subject to limitations justified on grounds of public policy, public security or public health—

   (a)   to accept offers of employment actually made;

   (b)   to move freely within the territory of Member States for this purpose;

(c) to stay in a Member State for the purpose of employment in accordance with the provisions governing the employment of nationals of that State laid down by law, regulation or administrative action;

(d) to remain in the territory of a Member State after having been employed in that State, subject to conditions which shall be embodied in implementing regulations to be drawn up by the Commission.

(4) The provisions of this Article shall not apply to employment in the public sector."

Article 45 TFEU is directly effective (*Royer* [1977]), both vertically against a Member State and horizontally, against employers (*Clean Car Autoservice* [1998]) and can be invoked in conjunction with other substantive EU law rights, particularly those pertaining to citizenship (*L.N. v Styrelsen for Videregående Uddannelser og Uddannelsesstøtte* [2013].

Free movement and its associated Union rights are not unconditional. Some restrictions apply:

- A worker must exercise his Union right to free movement in order to benefit from employment rights in another Member State. Union rights do not apply if a worker moves from one region of his home country to another. In such cases, the relevant national law applies (*R v Saunders* [1979] and *Morson and Jhabjan* [1982]).
- Member States may also restrict access to employment of other Member State nationals on the grounds of public policy, public security and public health (art.45(3) TFEU and Directive 2004/38).
- Member States may reserve access to employment in the public service to their own nationals under certain conditions (art.45(4) TFEU).

Under this last restriction, Member States may deny or restrict access to employment in the public services to nationals from other Member States. Because of the potential for Member States lawfully to extend preference to their own nationals and thereby discriminate against other Union nationals by classifying a wide variety of jobs as those within the public service, the Court stated that this exception should be interpreted strictly.

In *Sotgiu v Deutsche Bundespost* [1974], the Court said:

- Article 45(4) TFEU only applied to certain activities connected with the exercise of official authority.
- Since the employees concerned worked for branches of the government of the Member States, the legal designations of the jobs could easily be varied by the Member States themselves. These designations should therefore be set by the Court to prevent discrimination against nationals from other Member States.
- Article 45(4) TFEU only applied to access to employment, not to

conditions of work, once a person had been employed. If a person was sufficiently loyal or trustworthy to be admitted to such employment in the first place, there were no grounds for paying them less or treating them differently because of their nationality.

In *Commission v Belgium (No.1)* [1980] the Court reiterated that, like all derogations, the public service exception must be interpreted narrowly and uniformly, with a Union meaning. It continued, "for a state to justify excluding non-nationals the post in question must require a special relationship of allegiance to the state and the reciprocity of rights and duties which formed the foundation of the bond of nationality".

The requirement for such posts to possess such allegiance and to depend upon the bond of nationality was two-fold:

(1) The posts must involve participation in the exercise of powers conferred by public law; and
(2) They must entail duties designed to safeguard the general interests of the state.

The approach taken was functional—the nature and character of the posts were important rather than their titles.

In 1988 the Commission published a document setting out some guidance on employment which it considered would not fall within the exception ([1988] O.J. C72/2). These covered posts in public health services, teaching in state schools, research for non-military purposes and public bodies responsible for administering commercial services. What would continue to be within the public service exception would be members of the armed forces, police and judiciary. There has obviously been tension in this area of law. Member States believe this is an area where a state should be able to exercise its full sovereignty and employ who they wish to serve the state without having to abide by Union rules of non-discrimination. The Commission has attempted to balance this understandable desire by setting out jobs which are security sensitive as opposed to those which are not.

In *Scholz* [1994] it was stated that "public service would be taken into account" for Ms Scholz's application for canteen work in Italy. Although she relied on her previous experience in the German public sector, the Italian authorities stated that this must be public service in Italy. This discrimination was held to be unlawful as the job itself did not warrant it.

In the case of *Colgan* [1997] restrictions imposed on entry to the civil service in Northern Ireland as a management trainee were held to be illegal, disproportionate and not justified by art.45(4) TFEU.

The Union protection afforded also applies to those who move from one Member State to another to seek work. In *R v IAT, Ex p. Antonissen* in 1991 a Belgian national had entered the United Kingdom, but more than six months later he had still not succeeded in finding a job. The Court said that deportation would be allowed where an individual had been in a Member

State for more than six months, unless he could produce evidence that he was still seeking work and had a genuine chance of being offered employment. This principle now finds expression in art.14(4) of Directive 2004/38. Of course, it remains open to the citizen to invoke any of the other rights afforded under European law, in order to remain on the territory.

All the rights under art.45 TFEU and its associated secondary legislation are granted to workers and their families. The families' rights depend on their relationships with the worker and are thus described as parasitic rights.

WHAT IS A WORKER?

Neither art.45 TFEU nor the secondary legislation defines the term "worker". In clarifying its scope the Court has emphasised that "worker" must have a Union meaning inasmuch as it defines the scope of one of the fundamental freedoms of the Union. It must thus be interpreted widely (*Bettray v Staatssecretaris van Justitie* [1989]). In this and in other cases, the Court further interpreted the term "worker" (*Lawrie Blum* [1986]; *Raccanelli* [2008]). The criteria for qualifying as a worker within the meaning of art.45 TFEU are that a person:

- performs a service of economic value;
- for and under the direction of another person; and
- receives payment.

The following examples are illustrative of the interpretative issues faced by the Court:

- *Hoekstra v BBDA* [1964]—Although having lost her job in the Netherlands, Mrs Hoekstra was capable of taking another. The Court ruled that the term "worker" applied not exclusively to one who is currently employed, but to a person "who is likely to remain in the territory of a Member State after having been employed in that state".
- *Levin* [1982]—Mrs Levin was a part-time chambermaid working for wages below the minimum subsistence considered necessary in the Netherlands. As long as the work met the economic activity criterion, it did not matter whether or not the individual could support themselves on the money they earned.
- *Lawrie-Blum* [1986]—Miss Lawrie-Blum was a trainee teacher working under supervision but receiving remuneration for conducting classes.
- *Kempf* [1986]—Mr Kempf was a part-time music teacher who gave lessons for 12 hours a week. The Court stated that it did not matter whether the money used to supplement the income was from the individual's private means or from public funds.
- *Steymann* [1988]—Mr Steymann was a member of a religious

commune who undertook plumbing and general household duties for board, lodgings and pocket money, but not a formal wage. The outside work which he also undertook—a necessary part of the commune's self-sufficiency—was held to be a genuine and effective economic activity.

- *URSAFF v Hostellerie le Manoir* [1991]—The term "worker" was held to cover students on courses which required practical work experience in another Member State.
- *Raulin* [1992]—The concept of "a worker" included a person who worked occasionally under a contract with no fixed hours, but according to the needs of an employer.
- *CPM Meeusen v Hoofddirectie Van De Informatie Beheer Groep* [1999]—A person related by marriage to the director and sole shareholder of the company may be classified as a "worker" if he/she pursues an effective and genuine economic activity.

But in *Bettray*, the Court refused to accept that an individual who was working in a drug rehabilitation scheme was in fact a worker, because no real and genuine economic activity was taking place. The Court has been prepared to hold that art.45 TFEU can even apply to situations where the professional activities have only been undertaken for a short time and where, correspondingly, the remuneration level was limited, as long as the work undertaken was real and genuine (*Vatsouras and Koupatantze* [2009]).

ACCESS TO EMPLOYMENT

Regulation 492/2011 provides that any national of a Member State, irrespective of his residence, has the right to take up activity as an employed person and to pursue this activity within the territory of another Member State in accordance with the provisions laid down governing the employment of nationals of that Member State. In particular, he must have the right to take up any available employment in the host Member State under the same conditions as those allowed to nationals of that state. However, restrictions on free movement of workers may be accepted where such restrictions pursue a legitimate aim that is justified in the public interest and is proportionate to that aim (*Olympique Lyonnais v Bernard* [2010]; *Bosman* [1995]).

The worker is entitled to all the housing rights and benefits accorded to national workers. His/her children are entitled to be admitted to general education, apprenticeship and vocational training courses under the same conditions as nationals of the host Member State, as well as grants and loans (art.10 of Regulation 492/2011; *Casagrande* [1974]). The Court has expanded the reach of art.10 such that it permits the parent, who is the primary carer of the child receiving the educational service, to remain in the host member State, even where that parent does not have sufficient resources or comprehensive sickness insurance (*Ibrahim and Teixeira* [2010]). The worker is entitled to the same social and tax advantages and access to the same training in vocational schools and retraining centres as a national worker. Regulation 492/2011 provides other equal treatment rights for migrant workers such as Trade Union rights and housing rights (arts 8 and 9). Any collective or individual agreement regarding eligibility for employment, remuneration and other conditions of work or dismissal is null and void to the extent that it discriminates against workers who are nationals of another Member State.

The regulation therefore gives valuable rights to workers, in particular concerning:

- eligibility for employment;
- equality of treatment within employment; and
- rights for the families of those who are employed.

The material scope of the main sections of the regulation are set out below.

Eligibility for Employment

Articles 1–6 of the regulation allow migrant workers from another Member State the right to take up employment under the same conditions as the host state's nationals. This means that Member States must not specify discriminatory employment policies and companies must not operate such practices. In particular, they cannot discriminate in methods of recruitment, advertising vacancies or setting eligibility standards to apply for employment. However, art.3(1) allows Member States to impose conditions "relating to linguistic knowledge required by reason of the nature of the post to be filled" (*Groener* [1989]). Article 4 prohibits quota systems setting out what percentage of foreign nationals may be employed (*Commission v France (Re French Merchant Seamen)* [1974] and *Bosman* [1995]). Article 5 requires that similar assistance must be extended to nationals of other Member States in finding employment as is given to national workers.

Equality of Treatment within Employment

Article 7(1) of the regulation provides that workers from another Member State must not be treated differently from national workers—especially regarding payment of wages or salary, dismissal and reinstatement or re-employment if he/she becomes unemployed. Any discriminatory practices will be prohibited unless they can be justified under art.45(3) TFEU (*Schöning-Kougebetopoulou v Freie und Hansestadt Hamburg* [1998]).

Social and Tax Advantages

Article 7(2) of the regulation lays down that there should be no discrimination in social and tax advantages for workers. This covers matters such as a lower separation allowance for workers from another Member State and includes public service workers (*Sotgiu v Deutsche Bundespost* [1974]). This prohibition on discrimination applies even when these advantages are not related to a contract of employment, such as a war pension in *Even* [1979], and may remain even if the worker dies so that his family can benefit, such as concessionary cards for rail travel (*Cristini* [1975]). It does not cover social security benefits to which migrant workers are entitled only if they contribute to a social security scheme in a host Member State (*Frilli v Belgium* [1972]).

- In *Reina* [1982] migrant workers were held to be entitled to a special discretionary childbirth loan which was until then payable only to German nationals.
- In *Castelli* [1984] a payment made to all old people in Belgium but not to an Italian widow living with her retired son in Belgium, was also considered unlawful.
- In *Bernini* [1992] a study grant was allowed to a dependent child of a migrant worker under the same conditions as those applicable to children of national workers.
- In *Scrivner* [1985] a minimum income allowance was allowed to members of the family of an unemployed worker.
- In *Commission v Luxembourg* [2002] a Luxembourgish law providing for a guaranteed minimum income, but paid only to individuals who had lived in Luxembourg for at least five of the previous 20 years before application, was held to be indirectly discriminatory against nationals of other Member States.

Vocational Training

Article 7(3) of Regulation 492/2011 concerns vocational training. In *Brown v Secretary of State for Scotland* [1988] the applicant had obtained sponsorship from a UK company prior to taking up a university place. He then applied for a grant which was refused. The Court found that the course was not "vocational training" within the meaning of art.7(3) though it would constitute a social and tax advantage under art.7(2). This in turn was only available to workers fulfilling the criteria in *Lawrie-Blum*. The Court decided that Brown was not entitled to a grant despite his status of a worker because he "acquired that status exclusively as a result of his being accepted for admission to undertake the studies in question".

However, in *Lair* [1988] the applicant was a French national who had worked in Germany for five years and had requested a similar grant from the German government. Again, this was held not to be vocational training under art.7(3) but, because she had been a worker, she was entitled to social and tax advantages under art.7(2) even if she was involuntarily unemployed. However, the Court stated that a migrant worker who gave up a job to pursue further training would only be eligible for a grant when there was a close link between the work and the subject studied.

These difficulties are rendered somewhat nugatory by the judicial developments in *Bidar* [2005] and *Förster* [2008] since in both these cases the Court of Justice held that access to maintenance grants and/or loans for study now came under the purview of the principle of non-discrimination of art.18 TFEU. Nevertheless, potential students are required to prove sufficient integration into the host member state, in order to become eligible for said financial assistance.

RIGHT TO REMAIN

European Union nationals will be unlikely to exercise their right to free movement, if, after the end of their working life or operation of their self-employment, they were precluded from remaining on the host State territory. Thus, art.45(3)(d) TFEU and Ch.IV of Directive 2004/38 outline the right of permanent residence for workers and citizens respectively. Union citizens and family members gain the right of permanent residence where they have legally resided in the host state for a continuous period of five years (art.16(1) and (2) of the Directive). In calculating this period, time spent in prison will not count towards establishing residence (*HR (Portugal) v Home Secretary* [2009]).

Temporary absences for less than six months or longer absences of up to a year listed in subs.(3) of art.16 will not invalidate the claim for permanent residency. However, an absence of more than two years will revoke the right of permanent residency (art.16(4) of the Directive).

Article 17 of Directive 2004/38 allows for the right of permanent residency to be granted before the expiry of the five year qualification period to:

- retired workers/self-employed persons;
- workers/self-employed persons who are permanently incapacitated and unable to work; and
- frontier workers/self-employed persons.

The right is only granted when the following conditions are satisfied:

(1) Retired workers/self-employed persons. The individual has worked in the host Member State for the last 12 months, lived there for the previous three years and has now retired.
(2) Incapacitated workers/self-employed persons. The individual has lived in the host Member State for the previous two years and has stopped working because of permanent incapacity. Where the incapacity occurred as a result of an occupational disease or accident, the two year rule is inapplicable.
(3) Frontier workers/self-employed persons. The individual worker has lived and worked in the host state for three years, but works in another Member State while continuing to live in the first Member State.

In all cases, the family of the worker/self-employed person is allowed to stay permanently, even after the death or departure of the worker/self-employed individual (art.12 of Directive 2004/38). In the case of third country nationality family members, the article requires that that family member must have lived in the host state for at least one year prior to death. The family is also entitled to equal treatment as stated in Regulation 492/2011 as per social and tax advantages. Article 13 of Directive 2004/38 provides for the right of residence in the case of divorce, annulment and termination of marriage or registered partnership.

EXCEPTIONS TO THE FREE MOVEMENT OF CITIZENS

Directive 2004/38 and art.45(3) TFEU
Derogations set out in art.45(3) TFEU, in respect of workers, and the general provisions of Directive 2004/38 as regards citizens, provide that the right to freely move may be restricted on the grounds of public policy, public security and public health. The directive covers expulsion from the territory of a host Member State and sets out procedural safeguards which must be followed by public authorities if they seek to exclude non-nationals.

The derogations under art.45(3) TFEU only apply when a Member State considers the exclusion of an individual from its territory, but they cannot be used to discriminate against him regarding his employment once the individual has lawfully entered the country.

Public Policy and Public Security
These derogations must be:

- interpreted strictly (*Van Duyn* [1974]);
- proportionate to the objective pursued (art.27(2) of Directive 2004/38; *Bond Van Adverteerders* [1988]); and
- based exclusively on the personal conduct of the person involved. Previous criminal convictions are not in themselves sufficient grounds for taking any measures, such as deportation (art.27(2) of Directive 2004/38).

In *Bonsignore* [1975] an Italian working in Germany accidentally shot and killed his brother. This did not carry a prison sentence, but Bonsignore was convicted of possession of an unlicensed gun and received a deportation order as a general preventative measure to deter other immigrants from committing similar offences. The Court stated that such measures must be based solely on the personal conduct of the person concerned.

In *Bouchereau* [1977] a Frenchman working in Britain was recommended for deportation after he had twice been convicted of drug offences. Again, the Court looked strictly at the United Kingdom's reasons for deportation and stated that the public policy derogation may only be invoked where there is a genuine, sufficiently serious and present threat to one of the fundamental interests of society.

In *Adoui and Cornuaille* [1982] two French prostitutes appealed against the Belgian authorities' refusal to grant them a residence permit, despite prostitution not being an offence in Belgium. The Court considered that Member States may only justify restrictions on the admission to, or residence within, its territory on nationals of another Member State if it adopted, with respect to the same conduct on the part of its own nationals, repressive measures or other genuine and effective measures intended to combat such conduct.

In *Mary Carpenter* [2002] a Philippine national married to a UK citizen faced deportation for outstaying her original leave to enter the country. The Court held that the decision to deport did not strike a fair balance between the competing interests of respect for family life and the maintenance of public order and public safety. Ms Carpenter's personal conduct had never been the subject of complaint, the marriage was genuine and in those circumstances, the Court considered that deporting her would be an infringement of a right that was not proportionate to the objective pursued. By virtue of art.28 of Directive 2004/38, Member States, when deciding whether to expel an individual must now explicitly take into account factors such as length of residence, age, health, family and economic factors, the extent of integration into the culture of the host Member State and links with the home Member State. Further, individuals who have acquired permanent residence, have lived in the territory for over 10 years, as well as minor members of the family can only be expelled in exceptional circumstances (*Tsakouridis* [2010]).

In *Calfa* [1999] an Italian tourist was expelled from Greece for possession of drugs. Greek law provided for a lifetime expulsion from Greek territory. The Court held that such a measure was disproportionate. This situation is now covered by art.32 of Directive 2004/38. Under that Article, expulsion decisions must be reviewed after three years. The Court has also confirmed that Member States are now entitled to impose geographical restrictions on movement as an alternative to a total ban (*Olazabal* [2002]).

Public Health

Derogation from the principles of free movement of citizens on the grounds of public health may only be invoked to refuse entry or residence for the first time, since the Member State cannot rely on public health restrictions after three months have elapsed from the date of lawful arrival. However, Member States are entitled to subject migrants to medical inspections at the point of arrival. Such examinations must be free. Under Directive 2004/38, the only diseases which justify restrictions are those with epidemic potential according to the World Health Organisation or those infectious or contagious parasitic diseases which are subject to national law controls (art.29 of Directive 2004/38).

Procedural Safeguards

Directive 2004/38 also provides for procedural rights and safeguards which Member States must provide, especially if they seek to exclude an individual from their territory on the grounds of public policy, public security or public health:

- An individual should be notified in writing of any decision to expel/restrict movement under art.27. Such notification must be comprehensible to the individual concerned and must outline precisely and in full, the reasons for the expulsion/restriction, unless this would threaten state security (art.30 of the Directive. This article codifies the rights expressed in *Rutili* [1975]).
- In the case of expulsion, the Member State must outline the time limit by which the person must leave the territory. The Member State must allow a period of at least one month, except in emergency situations (art.30(3)).
- Individuals must be granted access to judicial or administrative avenues of redress, in order to appeal against the decision to expel or restrict free movement (art.31 of the directive; *Santillo* [1980] and *Gallagher* [1994]). This provision preserves national procedural autonomy.
- Where the individual appeals against the expulsion decision and applies for a suspension of that decision, the Member State must not remove the individual, except where the expulsion order is based on a previous judicial decision, the individual has already had access to judicial review, or public security requires his/her removal (art.31(2) of Directive 2004/38). Further, appeal against a decision refusing entry does not entitle the applicant to plead his/her case in person in the territory (*Geert Wilders* [2009]).

11. FREE MOVEMENT OF GOODS

Customs duties represent one of the oldest forms of national trade protection so it was hardly surprising that these and other such charges were one of the first obstacles that the Treaty set about removing to create a Europe-wide internal market based on unimpeded movement of goods across the whole Union. Ensuring the free movement of goods is an area of law illustrating how the Court and the Union legislators—the Commission, the Parliament and the Council—combine to attain a fundamental objective of the Union. The Customs Union is an exclusive EU competence (art.3(1)(a) TFEU).

This aim of establishing an integrated market can easily be frustrated by Member States practising forms of protectionism designed to shield their national industries from the competitive pressures of imports. The most obvious way in which this is done is by making imports more expensive or setting invisible barriers, such as different product, consumer and environmental standards. In order to prohibit these and other protectionist practices, the Functioning Treaty has identified three areas to guard against Member States erecting barriers to free movement of goods. The rules apply both to goods which originate in a Member State and to those which come from a third country and are in free circulation within a Member State.

Although the prohibitions restricting free movement of goods are addressed to Member States, the most important articles of the Functioning Treaty within the area of free movement of goods are horizontally and vertically directly effective (*Van Gend en Loos* [1963]; *Danske Slagterier* [2009]).

These three areas are prohibitions on:

- The imposition of customs duties (tariffs) and charges having equivalent effect to customs duties—arts 28–30;
- Discriminatory internal taxation—art.110; and
- Quantitative restrictions on imports and exports (bans and quotas) and measures having an equivalent effect to quantitative restrictions—arts 34–36.

CUSTOMS DUTIES AND CHARGES HAVING EQUIVALENT EFFECT TO CUSTOMS DUTIES

Article 28 TFEU

"(1) The Union shall comprise a customs union which shall cover all trade in goods and which shall involve the prohibition between Member States of customs duties on imports and exports and of all charges having equivalent effect, and the adoption of a common customs tariff in their relations with third countries.

(2) The provisions of Article 30 and of Chapter 2 of this Title shall apply to products originating in Member States and to products coming from third countries which are in free circulation in Member States."

Externally, art.28 refers to the Common Customs Tariff. Whenever goods cross an external border, the Common Customs Tariff is the same (set out in Commission Regulation 2658/87 which is regularly updated). Once it is paid, then the goods are in free circulation throughout the Member States. Member States do not have jurisdiction over the duty levied on goods from third countries. They may not amend the rate nor may they keep the proceeds which now belong to the Union as "own resources". Modification or suspension of the Common Customs Tariff is an exclusive Union matter and is decided by the Council. The Common Customs Tariff is one component of the general Common Customs Code of the EU. This Code was set up by Regulation 2913/92 and codifies the law and rules applicable in relation to customs matter across the European Union.

From an internal, Union perspective, art.28 means that Member States must abolish two types of measures:

- customs duties on imports and exports; and
- charges having equivalent effect to customs duties ("CHEEs").

Article 28 also mentions "goods", a term which is not defined in the Treaty. In *Commission v Italy ((re Export Tax on Art Treasures)* [1968] Italy levied charges on the export of its national artistic heritage. It was held that these constituted goods as "products which can be valued in money and which are capable, as such, of forming the subject of commercial transactions". In *Thompson* [1978] the term "goods" was held to cover gold and silver collectors' coins provided they were not in circulation as legal tender.

Article 30 prohibits customs duties on imports and exports:

"Customs duties on imports and exports and charges having equivalent effect shall be prohibited between Member States. This prohibition shall also apply to customs duties of a fiscal nature."

In *Commission v Italy (re Export Tax on Art Treasures)* the Court stated that in view of its fundamental nature there could only be express exceptions to this prohibition and such exceptions would be interpreted strictly.

What are Customs Charges?
Customs charges are taxes, duties and tariffs levied by the Member State whenever goods cross borders.

What are "charges having an equivalent effect to customs duties"?
The Functioning Treaty does not define this term, but it was held by the

Court in 1966 (*Germany v Commission*) to mean in this case charges imposed on imports of agricultural products in the guise of administrative fees imposed in exchange for tasks undertaken by the authorities in the interest of, and at the request of individuals. The Court ruled that they were still unilateral measures, imposed by the state of its own volition which, regardless of their label and the means by which they were introduced, had the same discriminatory and protective effect as customs duties. In other words, the name of the charge was not important; it was the effect that mattered. Accordingly, the action by Germany was dismissed.

The *Bauhuis* case in 1977 gave the most complete definition. The Court said that:

> "Any pecuniary charge—whatever its assignation and mode of application, which is levied unilaterally on goods by reason of the fact that they cross the frontier and which is not a customs duty in the strict sense, constitutes a charge with equivalent effect unless it relates to a general system of internal taxation applied systematically in accordance with the same criteria and at the same stage of marketing to domestic products alike."

Charges—no matter what they are called, or for what purpose—levied by a state solely because goods cross frontiers are charges having an equivalent effect to a customs duty, and therefore prohibited. The restrictive effect on trade between Member States of the Union that such charges engendered was prohibited.

In *Commission v Italy (re Statistical Levy)* in 1969 Italy imposed a charge on exported goods with the ostensible purpose of collecting statistical material to analyse trade patterns. The Court said that:

> "Any pecuniary charge, however small, and whatever its designation and mode of application, which is imposed unilaterally on domestic and foreign goods by reason of the fact that they cross a frontier, constitutes a charge even if it is not imposed for the benefit of the state, is not discriminatory or protective in effect and if the product on which the charge is imposed is not in competition with any domestic product."

The Court's attitude was:

- The Treaty was not to be circumvented by the form in which the charge was imposed (the form of the charge is irrelevant, the effect on trade between Member States is all important).
- The prohibition applied whether the duties were discriminatory or not.
- The prohibition applied whether or not the product on which the charge was imposed was in competition with domestic goods.
- There were to be no exceptions.

In the case of *Sociaal Fonds voor Diamantarbeiders v SA Brachfeld & Sons* (the *Diamond Workers* case) in 1969, Belgium levied a tax on imported diamonds which would provide social security benefits for diamond workers. Again, the Court emphasised that such charges were prohibited, irrespective of their purpose. The prohibited effect would constitute an obstacle to the free movement of goods.

What if a Fee is charged in Respect of some Service Given?

The service in question could be for a health inspection, a quality check or offloading charge. The Court accepts that a Member State is allowed to charge a fee for services provided to an importer. But such a charge is not to be levied simply because goods cross a frontier. It must be for services rendered before it is lawful.

However, the service in question must be specific and must benefit the individual importer, unlike the statistical information collected in *Commission v Italy (re Statistical Levy)* which the Court considered to be of benefit to the whole economy. The Court also took a similar approach in *Bresciani* [1976] where the question was whether an Italian charge for compulsory veterinary and public health inspections carried out on the importation of raw cowhides, was compatible with the Treaty. The submissions in *Bresciani*, as well as in the *Statistical Levy* case were rejected.

If a charge is for a specific inspection, benefiting the individual importer, then it falls outside the prohibition. But there is a condition—the service rendered must be mandatory. In *Commission v Germany (re Animal Inspection Fees)* [1988] the German authorities charged fees on imports of live animals. The revenue gained was to cover the cost of inspections required to comply with Directive 81/389. Under Union law, Germany was obliged to achieve the result set out in the directive by enacting its own legislation. The inspections were mandatory.

Charges for services authorised by Union law do not constitute charges having an equivalent effect to customs duties as long as they satisfy four conditions:

(1) the fee must not exceed the actual cost of the services rendered;
(2) the service must be uniform; that is applying both to imports and domestic products;
(3) the service is prescribed by Union law—a mandatory requirement— in the general interest of the Union; and
(4) the service promotes the free movement of goods.

These conditions are very strict. If fees are charged on any inspection which is not mandatory under Union law, this constitutes an obstacle to the free movement of goods and is unlawful. Charges which cannot satisfy the conditions are classified as charges having equivalent effect to a customs duty and prohibited under art.30 (*Commission v Germany (re Animal Inspection Fees)* [1988]).

DISCRIMINATORY INTERNAL TAXATION

This is the second of the three sets of provisions within the Functioning Treaty to guarantee the free movement of goods. These rules also relate to monetary charges levied by a Member State. Whilst arts 28 and 30 TFEU prevent financial measures in the form of customs duties at the borders of Member States, it would defeat the aim of guaranteeing the abolition of charges if a Member State could then discriminate against imported goods once they were inside the borders. Article 110 TFEU is the main Treaty provision to prevent a state from placing a fiscal disadvantage in the way of imported goods in competition with domestic goods, once they are within the state by ensuring that the internal taxation system of a Member State makes no distinction between imported and domestic products.

What distinguishes discriminatory internal taxation from a charge having equivalent effect to a customs duty is that:

- discriminatory internal taxation is imposed on both imported and domestic products; and
- charges having equivalent effect to customs duties are imposed exclusively on the imported products.

Article 110 TFEU

"No Member State shall impose, directly or indirectly, on the products of other Member States any internal taxation of any kind in excess of that imposed directly or indirectly on similar domestic products.

Furthermore, no Member State shall impose on the products of other Member States any internal taxation of such a nature as to afford indirect protection to other products."

Article 110(1) deals with imported products which are so similar to domestic products that they require the same tax treatment. The important point is that the goods do not need to be identical, they only need to be similar. The term "similar" has been defined as products which are broadly in competition with one another, "with similar characteristics and meet the same needs from the point of view of the consumer" (*Commission v France (re Taxation of Spirits)* [1980]; *Kalinchev* [2010]). If a product is judged to be "similar", then art.110(1) TFEU applies (*Johnny Walker v Ministeriet for Skatter* [1986]).

Even if a product is not judged to be "similar", Member States still need to be careful in their tax treatment of imported goods. Article 110(2) examines whether or not the domestic and imported products are likely to be in competition with one another and assesses the protective effect of the disputed tax (*Commission v France (re Light Tobacco)* [2002]). If the national tax law influences consumer behaviour to an extent which affords indirect protection to the domestic product, for example through crystallising the current consumer habits of the population, then the rule will be condemned. In this regard, the treatment of domestic beer and imported wine has proven to be a fruitful area of legal action (*Commission v UK (Beer and Wine)* [1983]; *Commission v Sweden* [2008]).

Article 110 does not prohibit internal taxation. Member States are free to set up systems of taxation which they consider most appropriate for each product (*Commission v France (re Levy on Reprographic Machines)* [1981]). What it does prohibit is:

● discrimination against imported products; and
● indirect protection of domestic projects.

Not only taxation, but the method of assessment may be discriminatory. Two different systems of taxation, one applying to domestic products and another dealing with similar imported products, cannot be justified (*Bobie v HZA Aachen-Nord* [1976]). In *Commission v Ireland* [1980] the tax was charged uniformly, but, whereas domestic producers were allowed several weeks' grace before payment was due, importers were faced with immediate payment upon importation.

Indirect Discrimination
While direct discriminatory taxation is easy to recognise in the light of the strict prohibition in art.110, indirect discrimination is less easy to detect. In *Humblot v Directeur des Services Fiscaux* [1985] French road tax applied tax on cars above 16cv at 5,000FF. It was established that France did not produce any cars with an engine size of more than 16cv so the disproportionately heavy tax affected only imported goods. In *Ioan Tatu* [2011] the Romanian pollution tax applicable to cars upon their first registration in Romania offered indirect protection to second hand cars coming from Romania.

Objective Justification
Even if a Member State establishes a tax system based on factors which indirectly affect imports more drastically than domestic products, the Court will allow a Member State to plead that there was some objective policy reason acceptable to the Union as a whole to justify its action. In this way, the Treaty rules are prevented from becoming too harsh. These reasons may refer to the use of raw materials, the processes employed in the production of goods or general objectives of economic policy of a Member State, such as protection of the environment or development of regional policy. In the case of *Commission v France* [1987] sweet wines made in the traditional manner tended to be produced in areas of poor soil and low rainfall and where the local economy was particularly dependent on wine output. It was therefore held to be objectively justifiable to give tax concessions in order to support economically weak regions. So, although there was indirect discrimination, it was excusable for France to use its tax system as a way of strengthening regional economies—provided that the concession was

kept open to all products, not only to domestically produced goods.

Similarly, in *Commission v Italy* in 1980 Italy imposed a tax on imported and domestic cars based on their capacity to pollute which was objectively justified on the grounds of environmental protection, although, in the circumstances, it imposed an unacceptably heavier tax burden on imported cars than on domestic cars. Conversely, the Greek Government was more successful in 1988 when it successfully defended its progressive car tax against the Commission's contention that the tax regime was unjustified (*Commission v Greece* [1988]).

However, in the later 1997 case of *Commission v Greece* concerning a Greek rule providing for a reduced rate of tax to apply to cars using "anti-pollution" technology which was not open to imports because of the practicalities of testing imported vehicles, the Court ruled that even consideration for the environment could not justify such discriminatory taxation.

The Relationship between art.30 TFEU (Customs Charges) and art.110 TFEU (Discriminatory Taxation)

Both Articles are complementary, yet mutually exclusive. A charge may not be examined under arts 30 and 110 at the same time.

In principle, if a charge is imposed exclusively on imported products, it is likely to be a charge equivalent to a customs duty. If a charge is levied on both domestic and imported products in a uniform manner, it is more likely to be part of a system of internal taxation. In *Firma Steinike und Weinlig v Bundesamt für Ernährung und Fortwirtschaft* [1977] the Court held that "financial charges within a general system of internal taxation applying systematically to domestic and imported products according to the same criteria are not to be considered charges having equivalent effect".

In order to distinguish which of the two provisions a charge is likely to fall under, the Court has applied a test based on the destination of the proceeds of the charge. The case of *Fratelli Cucchi v Avez* in 1977 concerned a tax imposed on the sale of domestic and imported sugar. The proceeds of the tax provided subsidies for both Italian sugar refineries and for sugar beet producers. The Court concluded that a charge, which appeared to be part of a system of internal taxation, could be considered a charge having equivalent effect to a customs duty if the following conditions were met:

- The sole purpose of the charge must be to finance activities for the benefit of the taxed domestic product.
- The taxed product and the domestic product benefiting from the charge must be the same.
- Any charges imposed on domestic products are made good in full.

These conditions are very strict. If all three exist, then it is a charge having equivalent effect to a customs duty prohibited under art.30 and not part of a general system of taxation which might, if it is discriminatory, be prohibited under art.110. In both cases, unlawful charges must be repaid by the Member State.

Enforcing the Rules

Since arts 28, 30 and 110 are directly effective, Member States may be called upon in national courts to repay any customs duties or other charges which have been found to be illegal (*Amministrazione delle Finanze dello Stato v San Giorgio* [1983]). Delictual liability may also arise with regard to breaches of arts 30 and 110 by reason of the restrictive effect of a charge on imports from other Member States (*Just v Danish Ministry for Fiscal Affairs* [1980]).

QUANTITATIVE RESTRICTIONS AND MEASURES HAVING
EQUIVALENT EFFECT TO QUANTITATIVE RESTRICTIONS

Abolishing charges on goods passing between Member States could not in itself ensure that goods moved freely throughout the Union. Member States began to put up invisible barriers to trade which were not easily recognisable and as such were a more serious threat to the free movement of goods. Such measures were also capable of restricting the free movement of goods to a greater extent than charges.

A Member State may infringe these rules by failing to act as well as by acting. In the Strawberry Wars case, *Commission v France* [1997], the Commission took action against France for failing to take all necessary and proportionate measures to prevent the free movement of fruit and vegetables from being obstructed by the actions of private individuals. Lorries transporting goods were intercepted, their loads destroyed and drivers threatened and attacked.

Contrast this with the case of *Eugen Schmidberger* [2003] where a peaceful protest on the Brenner motorway completely closed it to traffic for 30 hours. An action was brought against Austria, but in this case, having weighed up the interests involved (respect for the demonstrators' rights of freedom of expression and assembly under the European Convention on Human Rights as against the free movement of goods), the Court found that as the Austrian authorities had taken steps to minimise the disturbance, a fair balance had been struck as achievement of both objectives would not have been able to have been carried out by measures less restrictive to Union trade. However, completely banning heavy lorries carrying certain goods from a particular motorway will engender State liability (*Commission v Austria* [2011]).

Article 34 TFEU lays down the basic provision:

> "Quantitative restrictions on imports and all measures having equivalent effect shall be prohibited between Member States."

Article 35 TFEU prohibits quantitative restrictions and measures having equivalent effect to quantitative restrictions ("MEQRs") on exports:

> "Quantitative restrictions on exports and all measures having equivalent effect shall be prohibited between Member States."

Article 36 TFEU provides for derogations that the prohibitions in arts 34 and 35 will not apply because of specific justifications. These derogations are allowed on several grounds (discussed below) so long as:

- they do not arbitrarily discriminate against goods from another Member State; and
- are not a disguised restriction on trade between Member States.

Article 34 TFEU
Article 34 prohibits two types of activity:

- quantitative restrictions;
- measures having an equivalent effect to quantitative restrictions.

It prevents Member States from imposing a numerical limit on the imports of a certain product in an effort to protect their own products from competition from other Member States.

Although art.34 is addressed to Member States and concerns measures taken by them, measures taken by any public body, whether legislative, executive or judicial, as well as any semi-public body which affect trade between Member States, are prohibited (*Apple and Pear Development Council v K J Lewis Ltd* [1983]; and *Fra.bo v DVGW* [2012]).

What are Quantitative Restrictions?
These were defined in the case of *Geddo v Ente Nazionale Risi* [1973] as measures which amount to a "total or partial restraint on imports, exports or goods in transit". In other words, import bans, setting of quotas and the like.

What about Measures having Equivalent Effect to Quantitative Restrictions?
These proved more difficult to define. After some pressure from Member States and the European Parliament, the Commission issued Directive 70/50 (since expired) to clarify the meaning and scope of "measures having equivalent effect". Section 2 of this directive proved to be particularly valuable in setting out in a non-exhaustive list of what would be considered a "measure having equivalent effect to a quantitative restriction" with respect to national measures which apply specifically to, or affect only imported products. These are often referred to as distinctly applicable measures. Such discriminatory measures included:

- setting minimum or maximum sale prices;

- fixing less favourable prices for imports;
- lowering the value of imports by increasing its costs;
- setting conditions of payment for imports differing from those of domestic products;
- specifying conditions for packaging, composition, identification, size, weight, etc. which would only apply to imports;
- limiting publicity for imports compared to domestic goods; and
- making it mandatory for importers to have an agent in the importing state.

The directive also referred to measures which are non-discriminatory or *indistinctly applicable*, that is, applying to both imports and exports, but which may nevertheless restrict trade from abroad by, for example, setting disproportionately restrictive requirements on importers. The Court has developed its case law on many of these cases where it has established that the same objective can be attained by other, less burdensome means.

In *Procureur du Roi v Dassonville* [1974] the Court set out its own definition of "measures having equivalent effect" and addressed the double burden an importer may have to bear in that, having already complied with domestic laws, he may also have to change his method of production or documentation to comply with the importing state's laws. Dassonville had imported a consignment of Scotch whisky to Belgium from France, without the certificate of origin required by Belgian law. This certificate proved impossible to produce and Dassonville went ahead with the transaction, even going so far as to create a home-made certificate. The company was charged under Belgian law with the criminal offence of importing goods without the requisite certificate of origin and Dassonville argued that this contravened art.34.

The Court stated what has become known as "the *Dassonville* formula":

> "All trading rules enacted by member states which are capable of hindering directly or indirectly, actually or potentially, [*sic*] intra-Union trade, are to be considered as measures having an effect equivalent to quantitative restrictions."

This definition includes both distinctly applicable measures affecting imports and indistinctly applicable measures affecting imports and domestic products (*Ludwigs-Apotheke* [2009]; *Human Plasma* [2010]; *ANETT* [2012]; and *Petition for Judicial Review by the Scotch Whisky Association* [2013]). Thus, discrimination was not a necessary precondition for the prohibition to apply. The judgment also emphasised the effect of the restrictive practice, not the form it takes. The objectionable part of the Belgian law was that its effect hindered the free movement of goods. The Court continued:

> "In the absence of a [*sic*] Union system guaranteeing for consumers the authenticity of a product's designation of origin, if a member state

takes measures to prevent unfair practices ... *those measures should be reasonable* and the means of proof required should not act as a hindrance to trade between member states." [emphasis added]

The *Dassonville* case was fundamental in dismantling many of the obstacles by which Member States were endeavouring to discriminate against imports and protect their own products in the process of which they were infringing Union law.

A similar case involving labelling was that of *Commission v Spain and Italy* [2003]. The Court held that the requirement in those countries to alter the sales name of chocolate made according to Directive 73/241 in Denmark, Ireland, Portugal, Sweden, Finland and the United Kingdom was disproportionate and infringed the principle of the free movement of goods. Appropriate labelling would have been sufficient to ensure that consumers were informed and thus protected.

In *Commission v Ireland* [1982] the Irish Goods Council conducted a campaign to promote Irish products. The Court held that the campaign was in breach of art.34 as it intended to substitute domestic products for imports in the Irish market, the effect of which would be to restrict imports from other Member States.

Not all measures which promote domestic goods will be caught by art.34. In *Apple and Pear Development Council* [1983], although this body was set up by the UK Government, it was financed by fees paid by domestic growers and its task was to promote the consumption of apples and pears. It brought actions against some of the fruit growers who refused to pay the charge. The actions were defended on the basis that the charges were contrary to art.34. In its judgment, the Court stated that a Member State would be entitled to promote its own products, but that the marketing in question would be considered unlawful under art.34 if it was intended to discourage the purchase of imported products. Competition in terms of quality is desirable, but discrimination on the grounds of nationality infringes Union law.

In *Commission v Italy* [1991] Italian public authorities had to buy Italian made cars before they could get subsidies. This measure discriminated against imports, affected trade between Member States and was thus prohibited.

In *Tasca* [1976] Tasca attempted to sell sugar above the maximum price set by the Italian authorities for both imported and domestic sugar. While national law prohibiting price increases on sugar would not of itself constitute a measure having equivalent effect (indistinctly applicable), if prices are fixed at such a low level that the sale of imports becomes more difficult or costly than the sale of domestic sugar, then the Member State would be in breach of Union law.

In *Openbaar Ministerie v Van Tiggele* [1978] criminal proceedings were brought against Van Tiggele for selling gin below the national fixed price. The fixing of a minimum price for both imported and domestic products was not in breach of art.34, provided it did not restrict imports. However, it would be unlawful if importers were to be placed at a relative disadvantage because they could not make any profit on their products under these circumstances or because the competitive advantage conferred by lower prices is cancelled out. The Dutch law was in breach of art.34.

After *Dassonville*, the next major development was the case of *Cassis de Dijon (Rewe-Zentral AG v Bundermonopolverwaltung für Branntwein)* in 1979. German law laid down a minimum alcohol content of 25 per cent for cassis—a blackcurrant liqueur—though the alcohol content of the French cassis was only 15 per cent. Although this minimum level applied both to imports and domestic goods, its effect was to exclude French cassis from the German market. This measure was challenged by German importers on the grounds that it infringed art.34.

What emerges from the *Cassis* case are two fundamental principles of Union law. The first is the "rule of reason", whereby if there is no Union legislation on a particular topic, each Member State is free to take reasonable measures to prevent unfair trade practices. Prior to *Cassis* the emphasis had been on whether or not the measure had been discriminatory; now the rule of reason set out a non-exhaustive list of the type of measures a Member State may take, though these must be proportionate.

The second *Cassis* principle is that of mutual recognition. It states that if goods have been lawfully produced and marketed in one Member State, complying with the mandatory requirements of that State, there should be no valid reason why they should not be imported into any other Member State.

This judgment in *Cassis* built upon the foundations of *Dassonville* and meant that:

- in the absence of Union rules regarding the production and marketing of goods each Member State is free to lay down its own rules;
- which must be in proportion to the measure taken;
- but not if these rules have the effect of hindering intra-Union trade;
- and only if these rules were mandatory—in particular, necessary to defend consumers, protect public health, promote fair trade and ensure the effectiveness of fiscal supervision; and
- if the goods were lawfully produced and marketed in one Member State there must be clearly justifiable reasons why they cannot be sold in another Member State.

Cassis was also important because it removed the assumption after *Dassonville* that art.34 would only apply where discrimination between imports and domestic products could be shown and emphasised that market access was the main criterion.

In *Oosthoek's* [1982] national law restricted the distribution of free gifts in the interests of consumers. The Court stated that:

"The possibility cannot be ruled out that to compel a producer either to adopt advertising or sales promotion schemes which differ from one Member State to another or to discontinue a scheme which he considers to be particularly effective may constitute an obstacle to imports even if the legislation in question applies to domestic products and imported products without distinction."

In *Walter Rau Lebensmittelwerke v De Smedt PVBA* [1987] the Court ruled that a Belgian requirement that margarine should be sold in cube-shaped boxes in order to distinguish it from butter was disproportionate. Consumers would be sufficiently protected by appropriate and clear labelling of the product, rather than such a method which would be likely to hinder intra-Union trade.

In *Commission v Germany (re German Beer Purity Laws)* [1987] the Court held that German law stating that the word "bier" could only be used for products brewed in accordance with the country's special laws on brewing were disproportionate in that they went far beyond what was necessary to protect public health, the ostensible reason for the German legislation.

In *Cinéthèque* [1985] French law prohibited the marketing of videos of films, both domestic and imported, during the first year of the film's release. The Court stated that the protection of cultural activities constituted a mandatory requirement.

In *Commission v United Kingdom (re Origin Marking of Retail Goods)* [1985] the Court stated that a UK requirement to protect consumers by marking all goods with their country of origin would affect trade between Member States as such marking might encourage consumers to exercise their prejudices in favour of national products and avoid Union produced goods.

In *Commission v Denmark (re Returnable Containers)* [1989] the Court held that, despite special arrangements for importers as an exception to the Danish requirement for approved reusable containers, this national rule was disproportionate. The concession for limited quantities of imports was not sufficient to redeem the breach of art.34.

As a judicial creation, the list of mandatory requirements as first set out in the *Cassis* judgment is open-ended, allowing for new mandatory requirements to be discovered by the European judiciary. Indeed, the Court of Justice has seen fit to declare press diversity (*Familiapress* [1997]); cultural diversity (*Cinéthèque* [1985]); freedom of speech (*Schmidberger* [2003]); the environment (*Mickelsson and Roos* [2009]; *Commission v Austria* [2008]); road safety (*Commission v Finland* [2007]; *Commission v Italy (Mopeds)* [2009]; *Vincent Willy Lahousse* [2010]); and crime prevention (*Commission v Portugal* [2008]), all as mandatory requirements, in principle worthy of protection by the Member States.

On October 3, 1980, the Commission adopted a Communication concerning the consequences of the *Cassis* judgment ([1980] O.J. C256/2). It read as follows:

"Any product imported from another Member State must in principle be admitted to the territory of the importing State if it has been lawfully produced, that is, conforms to rules and processes of manufacturer that are customary and traditionally accepted in the exporting country, and is marketed in the territory of another."

Nevertheless, some cases relating to the retail sector illustrated the difficulties encountered in ascertaining whether or not a measure fell within art.34.

In *Torfaen BC v B & Q Plc* [1989] a retail superstore was prosecuted for violation of the Sunday Trading Act of 1950 which had the effect of reducing sales by about 10 per cent with a corresponding reduction in imports from other Member States. B & Q claimed this constituted a "measure having equivalent effect" within art.34. After some confusion as to what constituted a "trading rule", it was held that such measures were a "legitimate part of economic and social policy" and were designed to accord with "national or regional socio-cultural characteristics". The Court held that English Sunday trading rules did not therefore breach art.34 provided that their restrictive effect was not disproportionate to their purpose.

In *Ministère Publique v Marchandise* [1989] a Belgian law which prohibited the employment of workers in shops on Sunday afternoon was held not to be disproportionate to the socio-cultural aim pursued.

In *Stoke on Trent City Council v B & Q Plc* [1992] the question of English Sunday trading rules again came before the Court. It ruled that the Sunday Trading Act was within the prohibition set out in art.34, but that it could be allowed to stand provided its objective was justified under Union law and in proportion to the aim to be achieved.

However, the Court in *Keck and Mithouard* [1993] decided to "re-examine and clarify" its case law. Keck and Mithouard were convicted of selling goods at a loss contrary to French law. The Court stated that the *Dassonville* rule only prohibited measures that related to product characteristics and did not apply to selling arrangements, as long as the selling arrangements:

"Apply to all affected traders operating within the national territory and provided that they affect in the same manner, in law and in fact, the marketing of domestic products and those from other Member States."

Member States could thus determine their own measures to regulate selling arrangements where these would have no effect on imports and would not discriminate against imported goods. They would not fall within the prohibition of art.34. Conversely, measures which concerned the packaging of goods would fall within art.34 since they imposed a dual burden on the importer and such measures would need to be justified.

Keck thus limited the scope of the *Dassonville* formula. Under the previous approach, selling arrangements, such as restrictions on opening times, fell within the prohibition of art.34 and thus required justification under art.36 or the *Cassis* mandatory requirements. Post-*Keck*, such selling arrangements did not come within the scope of art.34 at all. Examples post-*Keck* included rules on the opening times of petrol stations (*Tankstation 'T Heukske and Boermans* [1994]), advertising bans imposed on pharmacists (*Hünermund* [1993]), requirements that baby milk only be sold in pharmacies (*Commission v Greece* [1995]) and selling potatoes at a loss (*Belgapom* [1995]). More recently, the Scottish Court of Session has held that a local authority rule requiring that passenger transport vehicles be adapted before being licensed as taxi cabs does not fall within the ambit of art.34 TFEU (*Spring Radio Cars Ltd* [2013]).

The clarification offered by *Keck* actually proved to be of only limited assistance. For example what would happen in the case where the selling arrangement rules and the product characteristics rules could not be separated from one another? Such a case occurred in *Mars* [1995]. Ice-cream bars were sold with 10 per cent extra free. The product packaging itself intimated this fact through use of an eye-catching flash. German consumer protection law considered the packaging to be misleading since the "10% free" advert flash on the product packaging was larger than the actual 10 per cent increase in size. The German restriction was a MHEE under art.34 and had to be justified. The German action was held to be disproportionate.

Further problems arose over the issue of television advertising. Total bans on advertising certain products will not be considered as simply selling arrangements and will be more akin to a marketing or product requirement, which would fall within art.34 and require justification (*De Agostini* [1997]).

In conclusion, the *Keck* clarification has been useful to a degree. Now, the vast majority of national rules that restrict where, when and how goods are to be sold do not come within the purview of art.34. Selling arrangements now only create a problem when they make it more difficult for foreign producers to access the market to sell their goods in the territory or cannot be functionally separated from product characteristic rules (*Fachverband der Buch-und Medienwirtschaft v LIBRO* [2009]; and *Ker-Optika* [2010]).

Exports—Article 35 TFEU
Article 35 reads:

> "Quantitative restrictions on exports, and all measures having equivalent effect, shall be prohibited between Member States."

So far most of the cases considered have involved national measures on imports. Article 35 relates to exports and applies in a similar, albeit weaker, way as art.34 does to imports. The principle of a Member State's action in hindering Union trade is the same, but art.35 historically required discriminatory intent to be shown, in relation to MEQRs.

For example, in *Procureur de la République Besançon v Bouhelier* [1977] a French law which necessitated quality checks on watches for exports, but no checks on watches which were to be sold in France, was held to be a measure equivalent to a quantitative restriction on exports.

In the significant case of *PB Groenveld* [1979] a Dutch law prohibited all domestic producers of meat products from stocking or processing horsemeat. This would avoid the risk of exporting horsemeat to countries which did not allow its sale. The Court restricted the scope of art.35 by requiring a difference in treatment to be shown. The Court stated that art.35 concerned:

> "National measures which have as their specific object or effect the restriction of patterns of exports and thereby the establishment of a difference in treatment between the domestic trade of a Member State and its export trade in such a way as to provide a particular advantage for national production or for the domestic market of the State in question at the expense of the production or of trade of other Member States."

This limitation on the application of art.35 was finally and curiously quietly dispensed with by the European Court of Justice in the case of *Gysbrechts* [2008]. A Belgian law that prevented Belgian online retailers from taking credit card details from potential customers before the expiry of the seven days cooling-off period available under the Distance Selling Directive 97/7 was deemed to be an unjustified restriction on exports since such a law had the effect of favouring internal online sales, rather than cross-border sales. In such a situation, the Belgian retailer would be more comfortable taking an order from a Belgian customer without a credit card number than a customer based in one of the other member States, since the Belgian retailer would find it easier to commence a civil recovery action for non-payment in Belgium. The CJEU in *Gysbrechts* deliberately chose to downplay the significance of this legal change, preferring not to highlight the departure from its earlier case-law, unlike its confessional ruling in *Keck*.

Derogations

Article 36 provides for exceptions to the fundamental rule that all obstacles to the free movement of goods between Member States should be abolished. The Court has stated that, like all derogations, this list of exceptions should be interpreted strictly. It will scrutinise national rules which discriminate against goods from other Member States before it confirms derogation. It will not extend the derogations beyond those listed in art.36. The list is exhaustive.

Article 36 reads as follows:

> "The provisions of Articles 34 and 35 shall not preclude prohibitions or restrictions on imports, exports or goods in transit justified on

grounds of public morality, public policy or public security; the protection of health and life of humans, animals or plants; the protection of national treasures possessing artistic, historic or archaeological value; or the protection of industrial and commercial property. Such prohibitions or restrictions shall not however, constitute a means of arbitrary discrimination or a disguised restriction on trade between Member States."

Article 36 is in two parts. The first part lists the exceptions to the prohibitions. The second part goes on to warn Member States that any derogation submitted must not be a means of arbitrary discrimination or a disguised restriction on intra-Union trade.

When a Member State claims that the measure at issue has been adopted under one of these derogations, it must establish:

- that it is necessary for the measure to be adopted—the test of necessity; and
- that the measure chosen was the least restrictive means of achieving the objective—the test of proportionality (*Elenca* [2012]).

Arbitrary discrimination means that the measure gives advantages to the marketing of domestic products—or imports—or exports from one Member State at the expense of another (*Commission v France (re Advertising of Alcoholic Beverages)* [1980]).

Disguised restrictions are measures which are ostensibly justified under art.36, but which have the effect of restricting the free movement of goods (*Commission v UK (re Imports of Poultry Meat)* [1982]; *Boehringer Ingelheim* [2007]).

Where the Union has already taken action to make sure that there are harmonising measures or standards set up in a particular area, Member States may not justify their own national rules which infringe art.34 and restrict intra-Union trade by pleading exemption through art.36.

The burden of proof rests upon the Member State relying on the derogation.

Public Morality

Member States may set out what constitutes public morality in accordance with their own scales of values. However, they must not impose double standards—one to prevent the sale and marketing of domestic products and another relating only to imports.

In *R v Henn and Darby* in 1979 the defendants were charged with importing "indecent or obscene articles" into the United Kingdom from the Netherlands. They successfully pleaded that this UK law was contrary to the free movement of goods despite the UK government's assertion that the prohibition on such imports fell within the derogation on "public morality". On the other hand, in the case of *Conegate* [1986] the seizure of sex dolls was not justified under art.30. On this occasion, the Court stated that because it was legal to manufacture these items in the United Kingdom—although it was subject to restrictions on where and to whom it might be sold—the UK itself was not in a position to restrict similar imports from abroad.

More recently, Germany was entitled to restrict the import of computer games into its territory, where the games had not been classified under the German games rating system, notwithstanding the fact that the games in question had already been approved by the British Board of Film Classification for UK distribution (*Dynamic Medien* [2008]). Thus, Member States are given a broad discretion to set their own morality standards, in the absence of EU standards.

Public Policy

Under this heading a Member State must show the imports or exports in question would be a genuine and sufficiently serious threat to one of the fundamental interests of its society. In *Thompson* [1978] criminal proceedings were commenced against UK citizens who imported gold coins despite a ban on such activity. The United Kingdom's submission succeeded on the grounds of public policy.

The Court has ruled on all other cases very strictly. What has been ruled to be inapplicable to the public policy derogation are measures that seek to excuse Member State action on the grounds of:

- avoidance of civil unrest which the national authorities were well able to cope with—*Cullet v Centre Leclerc* [1985];
- restriction of criminal behaviour—*Prantl* [1984]; and
- protection of consumers—*Kohl v Ringelhan* [1984].

Public Security

In *Campus Oil Ltd v Minister for Industry and Energy* [1984] the Irish government succeeded before the Court with its requirement that importers buy one-third of what they needed from the state-owned oil refinery on the grounds that without this revenue, the refinery would have to close down. This would mean that Ireland would have no source of oil to supply key national institutions and services in the event of a national crisis.

Protection of the Health and Life of Humans, Animals and Plants

The Court considers that the "health and life of humans ranks first among the interests protected" by art.36 (*De Peijper* [1975]). In *Commission v UK (re UHT Milk)* [1983] the Court accepted a justification that an import licence system was necessary to regulate the heat treatment of imported milk and to trace the origins of infected milk, but re-treating and re-packaging imported milk was an unjustified restriction on trade because milk from other Member States was already subject to similar controls before export. This requirement was simply a disguised restriction on intra-Union trade.

In *R v Royal Pharmaceutical Society Ex p. API* [1989] the code of ethics laid down by the pharmacists' professional body did not allow a pharmacist to substitute, except in an emergency, any other medicine for that specifically named in a doctor's prescription, even where the pharmacist believed that the effect and quality of the substitute were identical. The Court found this rule discriminated against imports but accepted the United Kingdom's justification as being on the grounds of public health.

In *Commission v Germany* [2008] Germany was entitled to impose geographical restrictions on pharmaceutical sales to hospitals in order to guarantee an efficient and safe after-sales service from a local pharmaceutical supplier.

In *Ascafor and Asidac* [2012] Spain was, in principle, entitled to request that certifiers of foreign reinforced steel for concrete comply with the Spanish quality rules in addition to those of the home state, before allowing access to the Spanish market.

The protection of the health and life of animals was successfully pleaded in *Bluhme* [1998], where, in order to protect the Læsø Brown Bee, the Court ruled that a Danish law prohibiting the importation of other live bees to the island of Læsø was justified.

Restrictions on the sale of extremely strong alcohol may also be accepted in light of the dangers posed to society (*Ahokainen and Leppik* [2007]). Further, restricting alcohol sales to the State monopoly retailer is acceptable in principle, as long as the national law does not further restrict the sale of alcohol through, for example, prohibiting individuals from importing alcohol through an intermediary (*Rosengren* [2007]).

Protection of National Treasures Possessing Artistic, Historic or Archaeological Value

Member States are entitled to determine the value of their national treasures possessing artistic, historic or archaeological value and may determine restrictions on their import. However, any protection afforded may not justify charges (*Commission v Italy (First Art Treasures Case)* [1968]).

In the mid-1990s, legislation was adopted to ensure that the free movement of goods would not increase illegal exports of such national treasures (Directive 93/7 on the Return of Cultural Objects Unlawfully Removed from the Territory of a Member State and Regulation 3911/92 on the Control of the Export of Cultural Goods (both of which have been periodically amended)).

Protection of Industrial and Commercial Property

This ground of derogation is controversial in that it essentially serves private aims, as opposed to public objectives, in that it operates to protect intellectual property holders. The Court of Justice has been circumspect in restricting the right to utilise this derogation. Since intellectual property protection has the potential to undermine the single market, through partitioning of national markets, the Court has made a fundamental distinction between the existence and exercise of the right. Thus, intellectual property owners may not exercise their rights where such action would threaten the coherency of the internal market. Secondly, the Court has confirmed that intellectual property rights are subject to the concept of European exhaustion, that is, once the owner has placed the goods on the single market, he/she cannot prevent further EU trade in the goods.

12. FREEDOM OF ESTABLISHMENT AND THE RIGHT TO SUPPLY AND RECEIVE SERVICES

Freedom of establishment and the provision and receipt of services are usually considered together because the right of establishment allows Member State nationals and organisations to set up in business as self-employed persons or companies in another Member State. It allows them to take up and pursue activities in a host Member State without discrimination on the grounds of nationality. These two rights, however, are not identical. Article 56 TFEU relating to services gives a temporary right lasting only as long as the services are provided and only if the provisions in art.49 TFEU on the right of establishment, a *permanent* right, do not apply (*Gebhard* [1995]). This dichotomy between permanent and temporary rights determines the extent to which the host and home State are entitled to regulate the behaviour of the provider of the service. These rights apply both to natural persons (individuals) and legal persons (companies). Article 54 TFEU applies the same rights to companies formed under the law of one of the Member States, with their registered or head office within the Union. This freedom also covers the right of so-called "secondary establishment" in another Member State, meaning the right to set up a branch or subsidiary of an existing firm or company in another state (*Daily Mail* [1988]; *Centros* [1999]; *Inspire Art* [2003]; *Cartesio* [2008]).

Some provisions of the Treaties relating to the freedom of establishment are similar to those already set out for workers, for example:

- Article 51 exempts any activities which are connected, even on an occasional basis, with the exercise of official authority (*Reyners* [1974]). This is similar to the public service exception for workers in art.45(4).
- There is also a right to remain after retirement for individuals who have established themselves in business with their families under Directive 75/34.
- The right of establishment and the right to provide (and receive) services are not absolute. Article 52(1) provides for derogations on the grounds of public policy, public security and public health which are elaborated in Directive 2004/38 above (*Calfa* [1999]).
- Directive 2004/38 covers rights for self-employed persons and their families to enter and leave the host state for the purpose of establishing themselves or providing or receiving services.
- There is no exact equivalent to Regulation 492/2011 which means there are no "social and tax advantages" as there would have been under art.7(2) of that regulation.
- Article 49 has direct effect (*Reyners* [1974]) as does art.56 (*Van Binsbergen* [1974]).
- Nationals of a third country, although residing lawfully in a Member State, may not rely on the Treaty provisions to establish themselves

in another Member State (*Razanatsimba* [1977]). Similarly, the right to provide services is limited to EU citizens already established in a Member State.

● Similar to the case of Saunders concerning the free movement of workers, provisions on the freedom of establishment do not apply to situations which are internal to one Member State (*Jagerskiold* [1999]).

THE RIGHT OF ESTABLISHMENT

Article 49 TFEU provides that:

"Within the framework of the provisions set out below, restrictions on the freedom of establishment of nationals of a Member State in the territory of another Member State shall be prohibited. Such prohibition shall also apply to restrictions on the setting up of agencies, branches or subsidiaries by nationals of any Member State established in the territory of any Member State.

Freedom of establishment shall include the right to take up and pursue activities as self-employed persons and to set up and manage undertakings, in particular companies or firms within the meaning of the second paragraph of Article 54, under the conditions laid down for its own nationals by the law of the country where such establishment is effected, subject to the provisions of the Chapter relating to capital."

Article 54 TFEU provides that:

"Companies or firms formed in accordance with the law of a Member State and having their registered office, central administration or principal place of business within the Union shall, for the purposes of this Chapter, be treated in the same way as natural persons who are nationals of Member States.

'Companies or firms' means companies or firms constituted under civil or commercial law, including co-operative societies, and other legal persons governed by public or private law, save for those which are non-profit-making."

The Union has taken a two-pronged approach to eliminate barriers to the freedom of establishment and the provision of services:

(1) Harmonisation of Professional Qualifications
The Functioning Treaty sets out that, in order to make it easier for persons to take up and pursue activities as self-employed persons, the Union would:

- take steps to carry out a programme of secondary legislation, namely directives, which would ensure the mutual recognition of "diplomas, certificates and other evidence of formal qualifications" (art.53(1) TFEU).

General programmes for abolition of discriminatory measures both in establishment and in services were drawn up in 1961 to provide for a wide range of directives intended to facilitate access by abolishing restrictions within the various sectors of the economy.

Originally, the mutual recognition system developed on a piecemeal, sector by sector basis, with architects, dentists and doctors proving to be the simplest professions to regulate and gain agreement upon. This system provided an almost cast-iron guarantee to the holder of the qualification that he/she would be entitled to practice in the host state. However, the difficulty with this approach was that it took an inordinate length of time to gain agreement between the Member States and in certain fields agreement could not be reached. Thus, by 1985 it was clear to the Commission that a new approach was required.

This new approach was more decentralised and inclusive. Directive 89/48 (Mutual Recognition of Diplomas) covered the mutual recognition of diplomas without harmonisation, but included a safeguard requiring an adaptation period in a host Member State or aptitude tests. Those who benefited from the provisions of the directive were those who could show:

- possession of a diploma indicating that the holder has the professional qualifications required for the taking up or pursuit of a regulated profession in one of the Member States in a self-employed capacity or as an employed person;
- completion of a post-secondary course of at least three years' duration, or of an equivalent duration part-time, at a university or establishment of higher education or another establishment of similar level; and
- where appropriate, that the holder of the diploma has successfully completed the professional training required in addition to the post-secondary course.

Directive 92/51 was adopted dealing with areas of professional education and training but which did not fall within Directive 89/48 as the persons involved had not completed diplomas or training for three years. As with the former directive the host state may require the diploma holder to complete an adaptation period of not more than three years or to take an aptitude test. Together, these two directives made up the General System of Professional Qualification Recognition.

With particular regard to the difficulties encountered by lawyers who had to undergo an aptitude test, Directive 98/5 was adopted to make it easier for lawyers to practise in other Member States. Not all Member States enthusiastically took on board the requirement to enact this into domestic law. In *Commission v France (re Lawyers)* [2002] and *Commission v Ireland* [2002] the Court held that, in failing to implement the provisions of the directive, both France and Ireland fell short of their obligations under the Treaty.

Directive 2005/36 (as amended) modernises, liberalises and consolidates the law surrounding recognition of professional qualifications (*Commission v United Kingdom* [2009]. Thus, under this consolidated regime, recognition of qualifications must be automatic in the case of seven sectoral professions (mainly various medical professions and architecture) on the basis of minimum training requirements and automatic for certain crafts, industries and commercial sectors based on the recognition of prior experience. In other professional areas, mutual recognition of qualifications is facilitated through the General System or through specific directives (e.g. the Lawyer's Directives). In these latter professional areas, the Member States retain the ability to impose additional requirements, such as testing, upon the incoming professional.

(2) Case law on the Principle of Non-discrimination
As there is no equivalent to Regulation 492/2011, and so no "social or tax advantages", the Court has construed art.49 in such a way as to outlaw national measures which give certain social or tax advantages to nationals (*CPM Meeusen v Hoofddirectie Van De Informatie Beheer Groep* [1999]), or to companies having their principal establishment in that Member State (*ICI v Colmer* [1998]) and which discriminate directly or indirectly against non-national, natural or legal persons. Similar case law has excluded discrimination with regard to the provision of services.

The Court has stated that the prohibition of discrimination is concerned with the rules relating to the various facilities which are needed in order to pursue an occupation. So by applying the principle of non-discrimination where harmonisation has not taken place in a particular profession, it has been possible to invoke arts 18, 49 and 56 to challenge traditional rules which discriminate against persons or companies from other Member States.

Both direct and indirect discrimination are prohibited. The Court has not hesitated to invoke art.18 to strike down national rules either in the form of discriminatory nationality or residence requirements (*Steinhauser v City of Biarritz* [1985] and *Commission v Italy (re Housing Aid)* [1988]).

The case law of the Court has also clarified the qualifications required for professionals to be able to practise in other Member States:

- If a person has already obtained what was recognised, professionally and academically, as an equivalent qualification and had satisfied the necessary training requirements, there should be no obstacle to his admission to a professional body in another Member State (*Thieffry v Conseil de l'Ordre des Avocats à la Cour de Paris* [1977]).
- In *Commission v Luxembourg (re Access to the Medical Profession)*

[1992] the Court ruled that formalities necessary to become a member of a professional body must fulfil four criteria in order to be justified:

(a) they must apply without distinction to nationals and non-nationals;

(b) they must be justified by imperative requirements in the general interest;

(c) they must be suitable for the objective which they pursue; and

(d) they must not go beyond what is necessary to attain that objective.

● In *Vlassopoulou* [1991] it was held that national authorities must consider any education or training received which is indicated by the qualification and to contrast that with the knowledge and skills required by the domestic qualification. If they are equivalent, then the Member State must recognise the qualification (see also *Morgenbesser* [2003]). If they are not considered equivalent, then they must go on to consider the knowledge or training received by the applicant through study or experience, which may be sufficient to make up for what was lacking in the formal qualification.

FREEDOM TO PROVIDE SERVICES

Article 56 TFEU deals with the provision of services as set out in art.57 TFEU. "Services" under the Treaty are those provided in one Member State for a person in another Member State. It has been held that the freedom to provide services is an integral component underpinning the creation of the Area of Freedom, Security and Justice (*Josemans* [2010]).

Article 56 provides that:

"Within the framework of the provisions set out below, restrictions on freedom to provide services within the Union shall be prohibited in respect of nationals of Member States who are established in a state of the Union other than that of the person for whom the services are intended."

Article 57 provides that:

"Services shall be considered to be 'services' within the meaning of the Treaties where they are normally provided for remuneration, insofar as they are not governed by the provisions relating to freedom of movement for goods, capital and persons. 'Services' shall in particular include:

(a) activities of an industrial character,

(b) activities of a commercial character,

(c) activities of craftsmen,

(d) activities of the professions.

Without prejudice to the provisions of the Chapter relating to the right of establishment, the person providing a service, may, in order to do so, temporarily pursue his activity in the state where the service is provided, under the same conditions as are imposed by that state on its own nationals."

Again the Court has played a major part in clarifying the scope of the Functioning Treaty provisions, in particular the prohibition of discriminatory measures by Member States.

In *HM Customs & Excise v Schindler* [1994] the Court examined the meaning of "services". Schindler was the agent of state lotteries in Germany who sent letters from the Netherlands to the United Kingdom enclosing invitations to play the German lotteries. The Court held that the letters were not goods but services in that they were provided for remuneration and offered in another Member State. However, lotteries and other gaming services, particularly online versions, can be legitimately restricted on public policy grounds (see also *Gambelli* [2003]; *Liga Portuguesa* [2010]; and *HIT hoteli* [2012]). More generally, the member states are permitted an extensive margin of appreciation to impose restrictions and limitations upon services deemed by them to be illegal or socially harmful (*SPUC v Grogan* [1991]; *Danish Satellite TV* [2000]; *Omega* [2004]).

Beneficiaries of both the right of establishment and the freedom to provide services include Union nationals, as well as companies formed under the law of one of the Member States. In *Commission v Germany (re Insurance Services)* [1987] the Court held that an enterprise would be regarded as an establishment rather than a provider of services if there was no branch or agency within the Union but only an office managed by an independent person authorised to act on a permanent basis.

Van Binsbergen [1974] concerned the representation in court of a Dutch national who was not allowed by national rules to have his legal adviser continue to represent him when the legal adviser moved to Belgium. In this case the Court set out the test of necessity and ruled that a residential qualification in a properly qualified person is not a legitimate condition of exercising that profession unless it is necessary to ensure the observance of professional rules of conduct.

In *Attanasio Group* [2010] the Court considered Italian restrictions on the minimum distance between roadside service stations to be contrary, in principle, to the freedom of establishment.

In *Karen Murphy* [2011] the Court held that national law which prevented the import, sale and use of satellite television decoding equipment that could be used to receive satellite signals from another member state was incompatible with art.56 TFEU.

In *Gebhard* [1995] the Court gave further guidance on the compatibility of national rules with the Treaty and reiterated the four criteria set out in

Commission v Luxembourg (re Access to the Medical Profession) [1992], which were considered under freedom of establishment (above). In other words, where national measures restrict one of the Treaty's fundamental freedoms they must be non-discriminatory, be able to be justified in the general interest, be objectively necessary and in proportion to their objective.

In *Bickel and Franz* [1998] an Italian refusal to use the German language in criminal proceedings for non-German speaking Union nationals staying in Italy was unjustified with regard to the objective pursued and would constitute discrimination.

In *Commission v Belgium* [2012] the Court of Justice condemned a Belgian law which required self-employed individuals, established in another Member State, to provide certain information to the Belgian authorities before being entitled to provide services.

The concept of services also extends to the recipients of services. Although the original Treaties made no express reference to the receipt of services, in the 1970s, Directive 73/148/EEC provided for the right of member State nationals to go to another Member State. Following the repeal of this directive and enactment of the Citizenship Directive (Directive 2004/38) this specific right is now superfluous given that EU citizens have the general right to leave their member State and enter another Member State.

In *Luisi and Carbone v Ministero del Tesoro* [1984] the Court held that the freedom to provide services includes the freedom for a national of another Member State to receive services under the same conditions as nationals of the host state. The principle of non-discrimination applies to the recipient of services (*Cowan v Trésor Public* [1989]; *Wood* [2008]). In the case of medical services, it has been held that UK nationals have the right to receive medical treatment outside the United Kingdom, where there has been an inordinate delay in receiving treatment on the NHS and to receive reimbursement of the costs incurred (*Watts* [2006]).

In *Commission v Italy (re Museum Charges)* [2003] Italian legislation on preferential rates for entry to national museums allowed only to Italian nationals and persons aged over 60 or 65 years resident within the area was ruled as infringing the principles of free movement of services and non-discrimination.

The Court has also held that it is a violation of freedom of services law for national law to require a recipient of services to withhold tax from the payment made to the service provider, where that service provider is located outwith the territory (*X NV* [2012]).

As regards education, in *Gravier v City of Liège* [1985] a French national challenged the Belgian fee for a vocational course as discriminatory and constituting an obstacle to her Union right to vocational education. This was followed in 1988 by *Blaizot* establishing that all courses, save those intended to improve the general education of students rather than prepare them for employment, are considered as vocational courses. The entitlement to loans and grants, however, is still limited to workers and their families as "social and tax advantages" under Regulation 492/2011, or to students with a right of permanent residence (*Bidar* [2005] and *Förster* [2008]). The scope of the right to an educational grant cannot be restricted to courses offered in the host Member State which are allied to a prior course of study (*Morgan* [2007]).

At the end of 2006, the Commission finally secured agreement on a new Services Directive, Directive 2006/123. This new law, in particular, requires the Member States to simplify their formalities applicable to access to services and to create a point of single contact, in relation to the formalities surrounding services. Information on services should be made easily available to potential recipients and providers of services. The Directive also abolished the formal rule that services are governed by the law of the home state and provided for a number of instances of host state control.

13. COMPETITION LAW AND POLICY

One of the most important tasks of the Union is to create and operate the Internal Market. Article 3(3) TEU further provides that this internal market objective is to be based on working towards a further 14 objectives. Of particular note is the reference to a highly competitive social market economy. This Internal Market is to comprise an area without internal frontiers in which the free movement of goods, persons, services and capital is ensured in accordance with the provisions of the Treaties. This definition of the Internal Market illustrates the original economic objectives of the European Union. As a result, the primary means of achieving this aim was to dismantle governmental barriers to trade, such as customs duties, discriminatory taxation and quantitative restrictions.

However, whilst recognising that dismantling Member States' barriers against competition from goods from other Member States was necessary to create an Internal Market, this would not on its own be sufficient if businesses were allowed to distort the market to their advantage and to the disadvantage of competitors and consumers. Businesses could easily re-erect commercial barriers to trade. Thus, art.3(1)(b) of the Functioning Treaty on the Functioning of the European Union provides that the Union has the exclusive competence to enact competition laws designed to assist the functioning of the internal market. Two fundamental objectives of the Union—market integration and the promotion of competitive markets within the Union itself—are thus incorporated within the Treaty.

The objectives of European competition policy incorporate equality or fairness. The EU law rules relating to state aid, for example, ensure that Member States do not favour their own national industries by providing monetary or fiscal advantages to them alone and not to competitors from other Member States. Any such subsidies must be compatible with the state aid provisions as set out in the Functioning Treaty.

The Union is also a major world trading bloc. Because the size and sophistication of the companies within the Union who are seeking to enter this global market can differ markedly, it is in the Union's interest that economic integration proceeds as speedily and efficiently as possible to bring prosperity to its manufacturing and service industries. Competition policy, therefore, also seeks to create and maintain a healthy competitive economic base and, in particular, to encourage the growth of small and medium-sized enterprises ("SMEs") which are economically valuable both to their own Member State and to the Union as a whole, as well as encouraging an "enterprise culture" within Europe. Legal certainty within the small-business Union is also recognised as essential to a competitive market.

The importance of protecting consumers—whether as retailers acquiring goods for re-sale or users of the end product—from the effects of anti-competitive conduct is also recognised. The Functioning Treaty sets out at art.101(3) that consumers should receive a fair share of the benefit of any agreements made between businesses. This can range from a greater variety of products, improved service or guaranteed facilities to more retail outlets for the goods in question.

By promoting a healthy competitive culture within Europe and thus encouraging efficient production and effective allocation of goods and services between Member States and as part of a wider market, efficiency is also recognised as being one of the major aims of competition policy. However, Union competition rules are not designed to promote efficiency at all costs. If this were so, it would protect the most efficient companies at all times and eliminate small and less efficient firms from potential new markets. In turn this would have an adverse effect on the objectives of integration, competitiveness and fairness. What the Union is concerned with is the structural behaviour of undertakings in a market and eliminating barriers to entry for new and potential entrants; legal, fiscal, historical and cultural barriers. Thus, the competition rules are concerned with the control of dominance within a market, the methods by which undertakings acquire and hold on to market power and the degree of interaction taking place between firms.

Because competition policy is dynamic, existing within an intensely economic and political environment, it has evolved from minimal provisions in the original EEC Treaty, through the case law of the Court of Justice and the developing institutional awareness of the Commission into a mature and comprehensive system of rules applying throughout an increasing number of industrial and service sectors of the Union's economy.

Thus, European Union competition rules seek to contribute to the promotion of market integration, to the strengthening of consumer protection and to the maximisation of economic performance within Member States. Competition policy is therefore central to the establishment and maintenance of an open market economy, enabling business and industry throughout the European Union to compete effectively and efficiently in the global arena (*Telia Sonera* [2011]).

The main provisions of the Functioning Treaty relating to competition policy are art.101, which aims to control anti-competitive practices, such as agreements which prevent, restrict or distort competition, and art.102, preventing undertakings from abusing a dominant position. Certain forms of anti-competitive conduct may infringe both articles, since arts 101 and 102 are not mutually exclusive (*Unilever Bestfoods v Commission* [2006]; *Hoffmann La Roche* [1979]). These two articles complement others to control government intervention aimed at sheltering national industries, such as those found in arts 107–109 TFEU relating to state aid and art.106 TFEU covering publicly controlled undertakings.

These rules are supplemented by secondary legislation to reinforce and expand the outline Functioning Treaty provisions, notably Regulation 139/2004, the Merger Regulation. This regulation prohibits concentrations between companies which would significantly impede effective competition in the common market or in a substantial part of it, in particular as a result of the creation or strengthening of a dominant position.

Concentrations falling within the threshold limits of the regulation must be notified to the Commission for prior approval.

Not only do the competition rules apply to companies operating anti-competitively within Member States, but also to parent companies located outside the EU and their European subsidiaries (*Istituto Chemioterapico Italiano SpA and Commercial Solvents Corporation v Commission* [1973]) and to agreements made between non-EU companies if their practices were implemented in the Union (*Ahlström (A) Oy v Commission* [1993]).

Through Directorate-General Competition, the Commission still plays a key role in the enforcement of the Union's rules on competition within the Member States and can instigate proceedings for infringements of competition law. In accordance with Regulation 1/2003, the Commission and the national competition authorities have extensive powers of investigation and enforcement (see below).

Infringement of the competition rules may incur severe financial penalties, particularly in the case where undertakings horizontally co-operate in a cartel. To date, the largest ever fine in respect of a cartel is that imposed on the Cathode Ray Tube cartel in December 2012. The cumulative total of the fine was €1.47 billion (IP/12/1317). In 2009, Intel was fined €1.08 billion for abusing its dominant position (IP/09/745). The Commission is entitled to levy fines of up to 10 per cent of global turnover for the preceding financial year whichever is the greater (including all group turnover), for intentional or negligent infringement of arts 101 and 102. It may therefore be assumed that the deterrent effect of disregarding the Union's competition rules is considerable. In fixing the amount of the fine, the Commission will have regard both to the gravity and duration of the infringement (*Group Danone v Commission* [2007]; *Commission Notice on immunity from fines and reduction of fines in cartel cases* [2006] O.J. C 298/11; *Guidelines on the method of setting fines imposed pursuant to Article 23(2)(a) of Regulation 1/2003* [2006] O.J. C 210/02). In addition, private enforcement of competition law by way of damages actions in the national courts is playing an increasingly important role in deterring companies from acting anti-competitively (*Courage v Crehan* [2001]; *Manfredi* [2006]; *Proposal for a Directive on damages under national law*, Com (2013) 404 final).

Article 101 is directly effective in its entirety (Regulation 1/2003).

ARTICLE 101 TFEU

Article 101 prohibits collusive behaviour between undertakings which would have an effect on competition and affect trade between Member States. The article itself is in three parts. Article 101(1) sets out the prohibited conduct, art.101(2) the consequences of indulging in such anti-competitive behaviour and art.101(3) allows the Commission, national courts and national competition authorities to exempt agreements under certain conditions. It reads as follows:

"(1) The following shall be prohibited as incompatible with the internal market: all agreements between undertakings, decisions by associations of undertakings and concerted practices which may affect trade between Member States and which have as their object or effect the prevention, restriction or distortion of competition within the common market, and in particular those which—
    (a) directly or indirectly fix purchase or selling prices of any other trading conditions;
    (b) limit or control production, markets, technical development, or investment;
    (c) share markets or sources of supply;
    (d) apply dissimilar conditions to equivalent transactions with other trading parties, thereby placing them at a competitive disadvantage;
    (e) make the conclusion of contracts subject to acceptance by the other parties of supplementary obligations which, by their nature or according to commercial usage, have no connection with the subject of such contracts.
(2) Any agreements or decisions prohibited pursuant to this Article shall be automatically void.
(3) The provisions of paragraph (1) may, however, be declared inapplicable in the case of:
    —any agreement or category of agreements between undertakings;
    —any decision or category of decisions by associations of undertakings;
    —any concerted practice or category of concerted practices,
which contributes to improving the production or distribution of goods or to promoting technical or economic progress, while allowing consumers a fair share of the resulting benefit, and which does not:
    (a) impose on the undertakings concerned restrictions which are not indispensable to the attainment of these objectives;
    (b) afford such undertakings the possibility of eliminating competition in respect of a substantial part of the products in question."

"Agreement"

The meaning of the term "agreement", within the context of art.101(1), is wider than simply a contractual obligation, whether written or oral. Even an arrangement between parties that is not legally binding may constitute an agreement (*Re Polypropylene* [1988]), as does a "gentleman's agreement" enforceable by arbitration (*ACF Chemiefarma* [1970]; *Power Transformers* (COMP/39.129 (2009)).

    Agreements may be "horizontal", that is between companies at the same level of trade or industry (the parties are all manufacturers or suppliers of raw materials, as in a typical cartel arrangement, or are all distributors or retailers) or "vertical", between companies at different levels of a trade or industry (a manufacturer with a distributor, a wholesaler with a retailer and so on). Both types of agreement may fall within the prohibitions of art.101(1) (*Société Technique Minière* [1966]), since both types of agreements have the potential to impede the internal market. Horizontal agreements tend to be condemned more readily by the Commission on the basis that they are inherently anti-competitive, whilst vertical agreements tend to be condemned primarily because of their tendency to negatively impact on the territorial integrity of the internal market.

Unilateral action taken by a manufacturer to refuse the supply of certain goods to its distributors has also been defined as "an agreement" (*Ford Werke v Commission* [1985]). The Court ruled that this ostensibly one-sided arrangement was so closely connected to a system of individual agreements between the manufacturer and its distributors that the unilateral action was part of the whole contractual framework between the manufacturer and its distributors.

"Undertakings"

In the absence of any precise definition within the Functioning Treaty, the Court has interpreted the concept of an undertaking widely to include any economic entity, company, partnership, sole trader or group of companies, whether providing goods or services, commercial or cultural, public or private. Examples of undertakings range from opera singers (*RAI/Unitel* [1978]) to port authorities (*Merci Convenzionale Porto di Genova v Siderurgica Gabrielle SpA* [1991]). The fact that an entity is state-owned or state-financed and provides a service normally provided by the state does not prevent it from being considered an undertaking if it provides services of "general economic interest" (*Job Centre Co-op* [1998]; *Compass-Datenbank* [2012]).

The Court will also regard as one undertaking companies that are ostensibly legally separate, such as parent companies and their subsidiaries, but which in fact are linked through ownership and management agreements (*Viho Europe BV v Commission* [1996]). In these cases, the Court applies the "economic entity" principle, judging both companies to be one undertaking when a sufficient degree of control is exercised by the parent to leave no room for independent management by the subsidiary. Agreements made between the two will then be considered as an allocation of functions (*Béguelin* [1971]; *Akzo Nobel* [2009]). Legal liability may also attach to successor companies (*ETI* [2007]).

"Decisions by associations of undertakings"

An "association of undertakings" refers to a trade association, federation or syndicate. An example of a prohibited activity would include the recommendation of prices even if such recommended prices were claimed to be non-binding (*Vereeniging van Cementhandelaren v Commission* [1972]), a non-binding code of conduct (*Publishers' Association v Commission* [1992] or compulsory training rules applicable to a profession (*Ordem dos Técnicos Oficiais de Contas* [2013]).

"Concerted practices"
Where two or more undertakings cooperate—no matter how informally—
on some coordinated anti-competitive practice, such as price fixing or
refusal to supply, such activities may result in investigation under
art.101(1). Even though no formal agreement may exist between the
undertakings involved, the Court has nevertheless defined "concerted
practice" as:

> "A form of co-ordination between enterprises that has not yet reached
> the point where it is a contract in the true sense of the word but which,
> in practice, consciously substitutes practical co-operation for the risks
> of competition (*ICI v Commission (Dyestuffs)* [1972]; *T-Mobile*
> [2009])."

This definition even extends to an individual instance of collusion (*T-
Mobile* [2009]). Although evidence of collusive practices between
companies can be difficult to establish, apparently inter-related behaviour,
such as price rises or other parallel conduct in itself will not necessarily
constitute proof of a concerted practice (*Åhlstrom (A) Oy v Commission*
[1993]). In essence, economic entities must determine their action on the
market independently of competitors, although this does not stop the entity
responding intelligently to the conditions prevailing on that market (*T-
Mobile* [2009]).
   In order to determine whether any agreements reached by undertakings
fall within the prohibition laid down by art.101(1), the Court has regard to
three distinct elements:

- whether the object or effect of the agreement is to restrict
  competition;
- whether such restriction applies to an appreciable extent within the
  internal market; and
- whether the agreement may affect trade between Member States.

"Object or effect"
The Court has ruled that there is no need to take account of the practical
effect of an agreement once it appears that it has as its object the prevention,
restriction or distortion of competition (*Société Technique Minière* [1966];
GlaxoSmithKline Services [2009]; and *Football Association Premier
League v QC Leisure* [2011]). However, if the object of an agreement is
clearly not anti-competitive, consideration will then be given to its effect
(*Delimitis v Henninger Bräu* [1991]). Examination of the agreement within
its economic and legal context will then take place to reach a conclusion as
to whether the effect of the practice breaches art.101(1) on the basis of:

- the nature or quantity of the products to which the agreement relates;
- the position and importance of the parties in the relevant product
  and geographical markets;

- whether the agreement is isolated or part of a network;
- the severity of the restriction; and
- the existence of patents, trademarks or other intellectual property.

"The prevention, restriction or distortion of competition within the internal market"
The list of agreements capable of distorting the structure of the market is set out in art.101(1) but is by no means exhaustive. The essential element is that collusion between undertakings capable of distorting the structure of the market has taken place. Distortion can also arise through the existence of an agreement between two undertakings and a third, which is not party to the original agreement (*Consten and Grundig v Commission* [1966]).

"To an appreciable extent"
This is known as the *de minimis* doctrine. Even though the wording of the Functioning Treaty indicates that any effect on competition and trade between Member States is sufficient to trigger the application of art.101, the Court confirmed early on that this must be "appreciable" (*Völk v Vervaecke* [1969]). Shortly afterwards, in the early 1970s, the Commission clarified this judgment by publishing a guidance Notice on Agreements of Minor Importance quantifying the *de minimis* threshold. The most recent Notice ([2001] O.J. C368/13) provides that agreements concerning goods or services will not be considered under art.101(1) if the market share of all the participating undertakings in the relevant markets does not exceed:

- a 10 per cent threshold where the agreement is made between undertakings operating at the same level of production (horizontal agreements); or
- a 15 per cent threshold where the agreement is made between undertakings operating at different levels of production (vertical agreements); and
- small and medium sized enterprises ("SMEs") are considered by the Commission to be rarely capable of appreciably affecting trade between Member States. The Commission considers that agreements between SMEs therefore generally fall outside the scope of art.101(1).

Nevertheless, the Court of Justice has recently confirmed that the de minimis notice does not preclude the application of article 101 if, in actual fact, the agreement has an appreciable effect on competition (*Expedia* [2012]).

At national level, the Court of Session has confirmed that art.101 will apply where there is an appreciable effect on both competition and inter-State trade (*Calor Gas v Express Fuels* [2008]). In assessing appreciability, it may also be important to take into account the cumulative effect a number of small scale agreements could have on the internal market (*Distillers v Commission* [1980]).

"Which may affect trade between Member States"
If an agreement is not capable of affecting trade between Member States—actually or potentially—art.101 will not apply. For the agreement to fall within art.101, it is sufficient that the agreement is likely to affect trade, even in the future.

If an agreement is made, *the effects of which are confined to the territory of a single Member State*, it does not fall under art.101, but is governed by the national legal order (*Hugin Cash Registers v Commission* [1979]). In order to assist companies in determining whether their agreement is caught by EU competition law, the Commission issued guidance in 2004 on the effect of trade concept ([2004] O.J. C 101/81).

Exemptions
Although an agreement has, or is intended to have an anti-competitive effect, it may be subject to an exemption from the prohibitions in art.101(1). In an attempt to balance the economic interests of undertakings, consumers and the Union itself with the desire to avoid unnecessary restrictions on business enterprise, art.101(3) accepts that some agreements, decisions or concerted practices which, although they reduce competition, may also have beneficial consequences which outweigh their restrictive effects, such as contributing towards improving the production or distribution of goods, or promoting technical or economic progress whilst allowing consumers a fair share in the benefits of such arrangements. As well as possessing these "positive" attributes, the arrangements made must also abide by two "negative" conditions. First, they must be no more restrictive than absolutely necessary in order to achieve the undertaking's apparent objective and, second, they must not give the undertakings the opportunity to eliminate any competitors (*Protimonopolný úrad Slovenskej republiky* [2013]).

Until May 2004, the Commission had exclusive jurisdiction to grant exemptions from the prohibitions laid down in art.101(1). Since then, the entire text of art.101 has been directly effective, that is, the decision as to whether agreements and decisions satisfy the exemption criteria of art.101(3) can now be taken by the competition authorities and national courts of the Member States, in addition to the Commission. The Commission has therefore lost its monopoly in applying art.101(3).

Block Exemptions
Under the old centralised system of enforcement of reg.17/62, the Commission was the only body authorised to grant exemptions to the prohibition of art.101. For administrative convenience, businesses seeking the protection of art.101(3) were required to individually notify their agreement to the Commission. After investigating the application, the Commission could prohibit the agreement or, if the agreement was acceptable, the Commission would issue a comfort letter or grant negative clearance. Further administrative pressure meant that this system did not reduce the workload of the Commission to the extent desired. Indeed, the

Commission often faced multiple notifications from businesses in the same industrial sector. Thus, the Commission resorted to using a general system of block exemptions, whereby the Commission would issue a prescriptive regulation for a particular industry sector which outlined the type of agreements which would satisfy the Commission. Businesses which re-arranged their operations to fit the rules of the Block Exemption Regulation, were generally safe from Commission interference.

In the latter years of its operation, the block exemption system came in for severe criticism. Essentially, the law had a strait-jacket effect, forcing businesses to conform to a particular model of operation in the marketplace. This approach stifled development and innovation on the market. Notwithstanding the criticisms levelled at the block exemption system, legal certainty has required that certain Block Exemption Regulations must remain valid until their expiry date. In addition, the Commission has continued to enact Block Exemption Regulations since the new decentralised regime came into operation. Examples of block exemptions in force include:

- The New Vertical Agreements Regulation (Regulation 330/2010) (which also extends to motor vehicle arrangements from June 2013).
- The Motor Vehicle Vertical Agreements and Concerted Practices Regulations (Regulations 461/2010).
- Technology Transfer Agreements (Regulation 772/2004).
- Horizontal Co-operation Agreements—Specialisation Agreements (Regulation 1218/2010) and Research and Development Agreements (Regulation 1217/2010) (as amended).
- Insurance Agreements (Regulation 267/2010).

In relation to the Block Exemption Regulations which deal with vertical agreements, that is agreements between businesses operating at different levels in the marketplace, it is important to note that acceptance of the benefits of vertical agreements by the Commission is a relatively recent occurrence. Vertical agreements typically involve a manufacturer and distributor. The benefit of the vertical agreements is that each business is free to concentrate on their particular area of expertise, leaving the other partner to concentrate on their area of expertise. However, vertical agreements have the potential to re-erect national barriers to trade since they typically involve a manufacturer granting geographically limited, exclusive or selective distribution rights to a distributor or retailer and often in conjunction with provisions restricting online sales. Such activities would impede the creation of a fully functioning European Internal Market by offering absolute territorial protection from competition from other Member States (*Pierre Fabre Dermo-Cosmétique* [2011]; *Peugeot Nederland v Commission* [2009]; *Nintendo v Commission* [2009]; and *Consten and Grundig v Commission* [1966]). Thus, the Commission has been keen to keep a close eye on such arrangements and hence has been reluctant to completely abolish the Block Exemption regime in this field.

ARTICLE 102 TFEU

Article 102 TFEU controls companies that are so economically powerful on the market that they can act with impunity, irrespective of what their competitors, customers or consumers are doing on the market. They are not only able to dominate the market in which they operate, but could also derive unfair advantages and eliminate competitors. Article 102 is directly effective and prohibits the following:

> "Any abuse by one or more undertakings of a dominant position within the internal market or in a substantial part of it shall be prohibited as incompatible with the internal market insofar as it may affect trade between Member States. Such abuse may, in particular, consist in:
>
> (a)   directly or indirectly imposing unfair purchase or selling prices or unfair trading conditions;
>
> (b)   limiting production, markets or technical development to the prejudice of consumers;
>
> (c)   applying dissimilar conditions to equivalent transactions with other trading parties, thereby placing them at a competitive disadvantage;
>
> (d)   making the conclusion of contracts subject to acceptance by the other parties of supplementary obligations which, by their nature or according to commercial usage, have no connection with the subject of such contracts."

Unlike art.101, which deals with agreements between one or more independent undertakings, art.102 primarily deals with the abuse of a dominant position by (usually) a single company, although collective dominance is also a significant concern under art.102. Although the prohibited conduct set out in art.102 closely corresponds to the examples set out within art.101(1), again, these are not exhaustive. The case law of the Court confirms that the open list of examples provided in the body of art.102 can be extended.

The prohibition contained in art.102 is absolute and admits of no exceptions. Article 102 comes into operation when three factors exist:

- a dominant position is held by one or more undertakings either within the internal market or within a substantial part of it;
- that dominant position is abused; and
- the abuse in question affects trade between Member States.

Once again, in the absence of detailed definition within the Functioning Treaty, the case law of the Court of Justice defines the terms.

"Dominant position"

In order to establish dominance, it must be established that the undertaking(s) in question are dominant in a particular market. This is usually taken to mean that the undertaking concerned "has the power to behave to an appreciable extent independently of its competitors, customers and ultimately of its consumers" (*United Brands v Commission* [1978]; and *Microsoft* [2007]).

Relevant Market

The first objective is to define the market in which the undertaking is alleged to be dominant. In other words, it is essential to identify the "relevant market"—what products constitute it and where the geographical boundaries of this market lie.

With regard to the relevant product market, interchangeability of products is the key factor in its identification. If a consumer can easily switch to another item, it would seem that, on the face of it, competition within that particular market has not been stifled and there would thus be no necessity for Commission intervention. To assess whether or not interchangeability of products exists, the Commission considers the characteristics of the commodities themselves and those of other goods that can be substituted for them. Products that only have limited interchangeability with others are not usually considered part of the relevant market (*Michelin v Commission* [1983]). From the Commission's point of view, the narrower the definition of the relevant market, the more likely it is that the undertaking will be found to be dominant in that market, while an undertaking would naturally prefer that an assessment would define the market broadly. The test is not set arbitrarily, rather an in-depth economic analysis of the market must be undertaken.

To evaluate the relevant geographical market, the Functioning Treaty states that art.102 will apply to conduct "within the internal market or in a substantial part of it". An assessment will look at the level of trading in one or more Member States compared to that in the Union as a whole. It is not necessary for an undertaking to carry out its activities in all Member States of the European Union—even activities in one Member State may be enough to trigger the application of art.102 provided that these had an effect on trade between Member States (*Michelin v Commission* [1983]).

In order to render its policy and decision making more transparent and thus enable undertakings to enjoy an element of legal certainty when drawing up their agreements, acquisitions and joint ventures, in 1997 the Commission published a Notice setting out guidelines to its definition of the relevant market ([1997] O.J. C372/5).

Establishing Dominance

Once the relevant market has been evaluated, the key objective is to establish dominance of that market. Several factors are relevant to the assessment of an undertaking's dominance.

Two major cases serve to indicate not only the approach of the Commission in establishing anti-competitive conduct under art.102, but the imprimatur of the Court of their findings. In *Hoffmann La Roche v Commission* in 1979 and *United Brands v Commission* in 1978 the Commission found that dominance would be considered:

● where large market shares have been in place for a considerable time;
● where the position of existing and potential competitors is taken into account;
● where an undertaking's share of the market was appreciably in excess of its competitors;
● where difficulties were faced by potential competitors trying to break into the market such as instances where customers are locked in to existing products and contracts; and
● where substantial resources have been expended on product brand image and advertising.

Collective Dominance

Although most incidences of illegal abuse of a dominant position relate to the activities of a single undertaking, art.102 also condemns anti-competitive conduct by "one or more undertakings". This collective dominance usually takes place when two or more undertakings, because of the economic links between them, hold a collective dominant position on the relevant market (*Società Italiana Vetro SpA v Commission* [1992]; *Compagnie Maritime Belge* [2000]). Such a market can often be described as oligopolistic in nature (*Municipality of Almelo v Energiebedrijf Ijsselmij* [1994]).

Abuse

Once it has been established that an undertaking holds a dominant position in a particular market, it is necessary to determine whether or not it has abused this position. Dominance of itself is not illegal. What is prohibited is abuse of the dominant position. The notion of abuse is an objective concept (*Tomra* [2012]; *Telia Sonera* [2011]). The Court has stated that an undertaking in a dominant position "has a special responsibility not to allow its conduct to impair undistorted competition on the internal market" (*Michelin v Commission* [1983]). Abuses can be characterised as exploitative (as to the consumer) or exclusionary (as to competitors).

It has condemned abusive practices, such as:

● excessive and discriminatory pricing (*United Brands v Commission* [1978]);
● predatory pricing and margin squeeze (*AKZO Chemie BV v Commission* [1991]; *France Telecom* [2007]; and *Deutsche Telekom* [2010]);

- fidelity rebates (*BPB Industries Plc & British Gypsum* [1995] and *Michelin* [2003]);
- tying-in practices (*Hoffmann La Roche v Commission* [1979]; *Hilti v Commission* [1994] and *Microsoft* [2004]);
- bundling (*Microsoft* [2007]);
- refusals to supply (*Instituto Chemioterapico Italiano SpA and Commercial Solvents Corporation v Commission* [1973]), including a refusal to licence intellectual property (*Magill* [1991]).

"Insofar as it may affect trade between Member States"
As with art.101, if the practice in question does not affect trade between Member States, then art.102 will not apply. Nevertheless, for the operation of art.102 to be triggered, it is sufficient that the conduct might affect trade even in the future (*British Leyland v Commission* [1986]).

Enforcement
Directorate-General Competition plays a significant role in the enforcement of the competition rules, alongside the new powers for national courts and national competition authorities to enforce competition law. Article 105 TFEU provides that, "the Commission shall ensure the application of the principles laid down in Articles 101 and 102".

In the past, European competition law enforcement fell squarely upon the Commission's shoulders. Successive EU enlargements, increasing calls for subsidiarity and an overly bureaucratic process for assessing the compatibility (or otherwise) of commercial agreements, resulted in the overburdened Commission agreeing to give up its enforcement monopoly in the early part of the 21st century.

In September 2000, the Commission published a White Paper on "Modernisation of the Rules implementing articles 81 and 82" (old) within which it set out its proposals for a Council Regulation to reform the rules on competition enforcement particularly in the light of the (then) imminent enlargement of the Union to the East. This new Regulation 1/2003 entered into force in May 2004.

Under Regulation 1/2003, national competition authorities, the national courts and the Commission have the power to apply arts 101 and 102. In particular, they can require an infringement to be brought to an end, order interim measures, accept commitments and impose fines or periodic penalty payments. National competition authorities are also empowered to apply any other penalty provided for in national law, while the Commission has the power to impose appropriate structural or behavioural remedies to bring the violation to an end (*Prezes Urzdu Ochrony Konkurencji i Konsumentów* [2011]). Articles 11 and 15 of the regulation provide for co-operation between the Commission, the national competition authorities and the national courts in applying the European rules. In order to preserve the pre-eminent place of the Commission in the enforcement apex, the Court of Justice has held that national competition authorities are precluded from declaring that art.102 has not been breached (*Prezes Urzdu Ochrony*

Konkurencji i Konsumentów [2011]). To aid consistency between national and European regulatory co-operative action, the Commission has issued a series of non-binding Notices (Notice on Co-operation between the Commission and the national courts [2004] C101/54; Notice on Co-operation within the Network of Competition Authorities [2004] C101/43). The establishment of the European Competition Network has also greatly facilitated co-operation in this area. In addition, the Commission also promulgated a Notice in 2004 that provided the Commission with the power to issue guidance letters in the case of novel competition law situations ([2004] C101/06). However, such guidance, coming as it does from an executive body, can only ever be of persuasive value to a national judge (*Inntrepreneur v Crehan* [2006]). The Commission has also issued a Notice on the application of art.101(3) TFEU ([2004] C101/97). Beyond Regulation 1/2003, the Court of Justice has confirmed that the Commission also has the power to institute damages actions in the national courts for breach of EU competition law (*European Commission v Otis* [2012]).

Devolving enforcement power from the Commission to national bodies was designed to free up the Commission's finite resources, allowing the Commission to concentrate solely on high profile anti-competitive behaviour which has a significant impact on the European internal market. In particular, the Commission is able to focus its priorities on cracking down on cartels. As part of this agenda, the Commission has instituted a settlement procedure for cartel participants, designed to coerce cartelists into fully cooperating with the Commission and effectively agreeing upon a plea bargain (Regulation 622/2008; and DRAM cartel Decision [2010] IP/10/586).

The adoption of a decentralised system of enforcement that involves a wide range of actors across 28 Member States creates the potential risk that inconsistency could creep into decision making, undermining legal certainty and the unity of the European Union competition law system. The adoption of guideline notices as outlined above, coupled with the duty of close mutual co-operation explicit in Regulation 1/2003, has greatly reduced this risk of legal uncertainty, alongside the fact that national competition laws now increasingly mirror the terms of arts 101 and 102 TFEU (*Allianz Hungária Biztosító Zrt* [2013]).

In order to fully enforce competition law, the Commission has been given wide-ranging investigatory and enforcement powers, alongside the power to impose penalties on undertakings. The main powers of Regulation 1/2003 are as follows:

Article 7	**Decision to bring the infringement to an end** Commission can, by legal decision, impose both structural and behavioural remedies, designed to both put an end to the infringement and to prohibit further anti-competitive behaviour in the future (*Güterman* [2010]).
Article 8	**Commission can order interim measures** Commission can order interim measures (as well as the Court of Justice under art.279 TFEU) (*Nováčke Chemické Závody v Commission* [2010]).
Article 9	**Commitments** Companies can enter into legally binding commitments with the Commission rather than face an in-depth Commission investigation (*Microsoft* [2009] (non-compliance of which led to a €561 fine in March 2013); *Coca-Cola* [2005]; *Visa Europe* [2010]).
Article 15	**Observations given to national courts** The Commission and the NCAs, on their own initiative, can submit written observations to the national courts (*Inspecteur van de Belastingdienst v X BV* [2009]; *VEBIC* [2010]). Oral observations can only be made with the permission of the national court in question.
Article 18	**Requests for information** Information may be requested from the undertaking, stating the legal basis and the purpose of the request, specifying the information required, setting time-limits and penalties for supplying incorrect or misleading information and indicating the right of appeal to the Court of Justice. A copy is sent to the national competition authority.
Article 19	**Power to take statements** The Commission has the power to conduct interviews to collect information. Officials doing so must inform the national competition authority who may accompany Commission officials.
Articles 20 and 21	**The Commission's powers of inspection** The Commission has power to make "all necessary investigations into undertakings" that is: (1) to enter premises, land and means of transport of the undertaking and of other natural or legal persons (where a reasonable suspicion exists that relevant information is being kept at that property);

Articles 20 and 21 (continued)	(2) to examine the books and other business records; (3) to copy and take extracts; (4) to seal the premises for the period necessary for the inspection; (5) to ask for oral explanations and record the answers. After consulting the national competition authority, and with its active assistance, the Commission requires to produce written authorisation specifying the subject matter, purpose of inspection and penalties for incomplete, incorrect or misleading answers, and the right to have the decision reviewed by the Court of Justice. The Member State shall afford necessary assistance requesting assistance of police or other enforcement authority. The national judicial authority shall ensure that coercive measures are proportional and neither arbitrary not excessive.
Chapter VI Article 23	**Penalties** The Commission is entitled to levy fines not exceeding 1% of total worldwide turnover for any undertaking that intentionally or negligently fails to comply with the procedural rules of Regulation 1/2003. Violation of the substantive competition rules, that is non-compliance with arts 101 and 102 TFEU or arts 8 and 9 of Regulation 1/2003, attracts a maximum fine level of 10% of total worldwide turnover (*Güterman* [2010]). In 2012, the highest collective fines were imposed upon members of the Cathode Ray Tube Cartel (*Chunghwa* [2012]). The fines levied are expressly not to be considered as criminal law sanctions (Opinion of Advocate-General Mazák in *Lafarge v Commission* [2010]). Member States are of course entitled to criminalise anti-competitive behaviour according to national law. A level of legal certainty in relation to the setting of fines is given by the Commission's Guidelines on the method of setting fines from 2006 (O.J. 2006 C 210/2). Ultimately, the Commission's wide discretion in setting fines is tempered by the power of judicial control wielded by the CJEU (*Chalkor* [2010]; *Hoechst* [2009]; *SGL Carbon* [2007]).
Article 24	Periodic penalty payments may be imposed not exceeding 5% of the average worldwide daily turnover (*Microsoft* [2012]—the Court of Justice fixed the original fine imposed by the Commission at €860 million).

Article 27	**Hearings** Before the Commission makes a decision on the merits of a case, it shall give the undertaking concerned the opportunity of being heard on the matters under dispute. The right of defence shall be fully respected with access allowed to the Commission's file, subject to the legitimate interest of undertakings in the protection of their business secrets. Further, art.28 of the Regulation provides that the Commission and the Member States are under an obligation of professional secrecy, in relation to business information collected during the competition investigation.
Article 31	**Review of the Commission's decision** The Court of Justice has unlimited jurisdiction to review decisions whereby the Commission has fixed a fine or periodic penalty payment. It may cancel, reduce or increase the amounts originally imposed (*William Prym* [2009]; *Microsoft* [2012]).

Although the Commission was previously under no duty to give advance notification of an investigation to an undertaking (*National Panasonic (UK) Ltd v Commission* [1980]), art.20(4) of Regulation 1/2003 sets out that the decision of the Commission to inspect an undertaking shall appoint the date on which it is to begin. Moreover, where a compulsory investigation is opposed, an undertaking's rights must also be protected by the procedural guarantees laid down by national law (*Hoechst AG v Commission* [1989]).

Compliance is enforced with the assistance of the "competent authority" in the appropriate Member State. In the United Kingdom, this is the Office of Fair Trading ("OFT") which can apply for appropriate injunctions/interdicts to enforce the powers of the Commission. The Commission copies all important papers to the OFT which comments on cases which raise important issues, particularly where UK interests are involved. Its representatives attend hearings in Brussels when companies make their response to the Statement of Objections issued by the Commission and they participate in an Advisory Committee on Restrictive Practices and Dominant Positions which considers decisions before they are made final.

Legal professional privilege may be claimed but not in respect of communications to in-house lawyers or lawyers based outside the Union, essentially on the basis that these categories of lawyer are not sufficiently independent and/or do not possess a sufficiently strong link to the principle of collaborating with the administration of justice (*Akzo Nobel* [2010]). However, the increasing regulation of in-house lawyers is blurring the distinction between in-house and independent lawyers (*Akzo Nobel* [2007]). In any event, the privilege only extends to information closely linked to the subject matter of the investigation (*AM & S Europe Ltd v Commission* [1982]).

Documents acquired by the Commission during the course of its investigations will inevitably be commercially sensitive. The Commission has a general duty not to disclose information on business secrets acquired by it during the course of its investigations (*AKZO Chemie BV v Commission* [1986] and art.28 of Regulation 1/2003).

Any information acquired as a result of Commission investigations shall only be used for the purpose of the relevant investigation, although national authorities are not precluded from relying on such information when deciding whether or not to initiate national proceedings (*Direcciòn General de Defensa de la Competencia v Asociaciòn Española de Banca Privada* [1992]).

In the event of the Commission finding a breach of the competition rules, an undertaking is not obliged to admit to an infringement and is entitled to refuse to answer questions if its responses would be self-incriminating (*Orkem v Commission* [1989]).

INDEX